MW00748009

STUDIES IN EPHESIANS

Ephesus, ancient and great, under Rome became the capital of Asia Minor. Under Paul's labors it became the center of Christianity in that province. Its greatest attraction was the temple of Diana, which ranked at one time as one of the seven wonders of the world. It was 342½ x 164 feet, standing on a platform 425 x 239½ feet. It had 100 marble columns, each from a single block of marble, 55 feet high, the roof covered with large white marble tile. It was adorned in its interior with surpassing splendor, including the works of Phidias, Praxiteles, Scopas, Parrhasius, and Apelles. The great theater of the city had an auditorium diameter, 425 feet; seating capacity, 24,-600; orchestra, 110 feet in diameter. Read Acts 19.

In this center of idolatry and luxury, the grace of God in Paul raised up a great church which became the center of Christianity in Asia Minor. Later, John the apostle came, here died, and was buried by the side of the mother of our Lord. Faithfully the church was warned by Paul (Acts 20: 17-38), and by John (Rev. 2:1-7). Note also the great epistle of our study. But city and church later failed. Our illustration shows the temple site covered by water and broken pillars.

RUINS OF EPHESUS

STUDIES *in* EPHESIANS

Suggestive Thoughts on the Wonderful Epistle

By

MILTON C. WILCOX

"That the God of our Lord Jesus Christ, the Father of glory, may give unto you a spirit of wisdom and revelation in the knowledge of Him; having the eyes of your heart enlightened, that ye may know what is the hope of His calling, what the riches of the glory of His inheritance in the saints, and what the exceeding greatness of His power to usward who believe."

(Second Edition)

TEACH Services, Inc.
New York

PRINTED IN
THE UNITED STATES OF AMERICA

World rights reserved. This book or any portion thereof may not be copied or
reproduced in any form or manner whatever, except as provided by law,
without the written permission of the publisher,
except by a reviewer who may quote brief passages in a review.

The author assumes full responsibility for the accuracy
of all facts and quotations as cited in this book.

Facsimile Reproduction

As this book played a formative role in the development of Christian thought
and the publisher feels that this book, with its candor and depth, still holds
significance for the church today. Therefore the publisher has chosen to
reproduce this historical classic from an original copy. Frequent variations in
the quality of the print are unavoidable due to the condition of the original.
Thus the print may look darker or lighter or appear to be missing detail, more
in some places than in others.

PREFATORY

This brief study of one of the greatest of Paul's epistles is, the author recognizes, altogether inadequate. The limit of the little book does not permit the development of the great themes of the epistle, such as divine foreordination, the mystery of God, Israel and the Gentiles, the church of the living God, the body of Christ, spiritual gifts, and other great features. But such as it is, it is sent forth with the prayer that those who read it may find help, and that the earnest student may find in the exceeding riches of God's grace heart and soul treasures that will be perpetuated in transformed character through all eternity.

CONTENTS

INTRODUCTION

That the apostle Paul is the author of this epistle there is no question among Bible believers. It was one of the four epistles of his first imprisonment in Rome. See chapters 3:1; 4:1; 6:20. The other three are Philemon, Philippians, and Colossians. Philemon 1:23; Phil. 1:7, 17; Col. 4:10. Both Colossians and Ephesians were sent from Rome by Tychicus. Col. 4:7; Eph. 6:21, 22.

Paul reached Rome after his shipwreck at Malta in the spring of 61 A. D., in the seventh year of the reign of Nero. Here he was guarded by soldiers, being chained to the guard on duty. His two years of prison life at Cæsarea gave him rest from strenuous labor and time for meditation and prayer. He sank deeper the wells of thought into the great mystery of God. He strongly emphasizes the mystery, the church of God, and Christ, the Head of the church.

The apostle makes no reference to the church in the great western city of Asia, Ephesus. He had a wonderful experience there of nearly three years. Acts 19 reveals somewhat of the thorough work of conversion wrought there under the mighty power of the gospel. See verses 10, 11, 17-20. All Asia Minor was stirred by the word. See verses 26, 27. Paul's work had made friends of chief men. Verse 31. The thoroughness of his labor is indicated in his talk to the elders of Ephesus and their love for him, as shown in Acts 20:17-38.

To mention individual names would have taken too much space in the great epistle. Paul set before the Ephesians again the great gospel.

The text used in this brief study is that of the Standard American Revised Version, considered by many devout Bible students the best, because based on earlier and better copies of the original, longer time given to its translation, and more uniform in its renderings. Others are referred to occasionally.

CHAPTER ONE

A Mighty Revelation: Analysis

I. The introduction — The writer and his greeting. Verses 1, 2.

II. The setting forth in one marvelous sentence God's great purpose for His people. Verses 3-14.
1. Before sin entered. Verses 3-6.
2. After sin's entrance. Verses 7-12.
3. His work through the word of truth and the power of the Spirit. Verses 13, 14.

All is wrought to the praise of the glory of His grace.

III. The inspired prayer that God's purpose and power may be effective in believers. Verses 15-23.

I. The Writer and His Greeting. Verses 1, 2

Paul,[1] an apostle [2] of Christ Jesus through the will of God, to the saints [3] that are at Ephesus, and the faithful in Christ Jesus: Grace to you [4] and peace from God our Father and the Lord Jesus Christ."

NOTE AND COMMENT

1. "Paul."— Formerly Saul of Tarsus. He was in early life reared a strict Pharisee, and later sat at the feet of the famous Gamaliel as a doctor of the law. As a Jew he was a zealot, and persecuted to the death the Christians, because he thought they perverted the law and were destructive to the commonwealth of Israel. But in his honest, though mad, career, God arrested him on his way to Damascus, revealed Himself to the greatly humbled man, sent him to an erstwhile despised disciple for further instruction, called him to be an apostle; nay, more, God would show him what things he must suffer for His name's sake. His experience is set forth in Acts. He stayed a while in Damascus, and then he went into Arabia, where he remained for two years or more in the study of the Scriptures and communion with God. The word does not tell us, but we may well believe it was near the Holy Mount where God instructed Moses and Elijah, and from which He spoke

His law. From this great experience Paul returned to his work. Paul therefore became the great apostle to the Gentiles, dropping His Hebrew name, Saul, and designating himself by what was probably his Roman name, Paul —"little." His later zeal was not surpassed by his earlier, but it was tempered by divine love. The one thing of his life was to preach Christ; the motive,—"the love of Christ containeth" me; the constant inspiration,—"the heavenly vision." "In labors more abundantly," in perils and suffering above measure, he fought the fight for his Saviour and God to the triumphant end.

2. "An apostle."— The word *apostolos* means one sent,— a messenger of Christ Jesus, one invested with the highest of spiritual gifts (1 Cor. 12:28), an ambassador of God, called to lead out in new fields in the proclamation of the gospel in the establishment of God's work. "The apostle deals with the whole body of truth. He has to state it, to systematize it; to make it available to the saints in order to their guidance and sustenance."— *G. Campbell Morgan.* **"Through the will of God."** The great apostle has high regard for the will of Him who controlled the universe. Six times he emphasizes it. God's gifts for service are not of man's choosing. There are many who prefer to be apostles, and prophets, and preachers, and strive so to be, with an ambition which will not be satisfied. No one is convinced of this but themselves. Sometimes Satan comes into the ambitious, unsanctified heart and deceives the man, and perhaps others, into believing he is what he wants to be. There is but one test for all manifestations and exercises; that test is the word of God and the fruit which is borne according to that word. God knows our limitations, knows what gift we can exercise best, and therefore He bestows upon every one, not as His children will, but "dividing to each one severally even as He will." 1 Cor. 12:11. Is it God's call? Let us respond. Is it the gift of His Spirit? Let us use it. Working in harmony with His will, the work is always both blessed and successful.

3. "To the saints."— The holy ones, those separated from the world and set apart unto Christ,— all true Christians. The word "saint" does not mean necessarily one that is perfect, that has overcome, that has won perfect victory in Christ. It

simply means one who has, in response to God's call, separated himself from the world and sin, yielded the heart to God to be cleansed, fitted, used by Him in His way. Over and over again the children of God, with all their imperfections, are called saints. They do not, however, call themselves so. Paul does not speak of himself as a saint. He exalts the gift which God has bestowed, by calling himself sometimes "an apostle." Sometimes the apostles call themselves "servants." They do not boast of their holiness, or of their perfection. They leave God to look upon them through His own righteousness, and see in them the character that is expressed in the motive of the heart, and which He will Himself work out if the motive holds true and perseverance does not fail. And so this epistle, with all its wonderful comfort, its marvelous depths of the revelation of God's goodness and grace, is revealed to the saints and to the faithful in Christ Jesus everywhere. And, reader, if we are among those, however imperfect we may count ourselves, if we have yielded ourselves to Him, to be all that He would have us to be, all the riches in this marvelous book are ours.

4. **"Grace to you."**— Unmerited favor, full of love and forgiveness and power. Grace is God's giving of Himself. He is "the God of all grace." 1 Peter 5:10. Ephesians has been called "the epistle of grace." **"And peace."**— How much the old warring world needs peace! How many hearts there are that long for peace! How many times hearts are disappointed in finding strife where they looked for peace. But God gives not as the world gives. The grace and the peace are from God. He is not at war with us; man is at war with Him. "Because the mind of the flesh is enmity against God; for it is not subject to the law of God, neither indeed can it be." Rom. 8:7. But the wonderful grace of God gave His Son to die, that the enmity might be taken away, and that His infinite love might win us to loyalty to Him. The grace and the peace come from both Father and Son. There is perfect union with Them. Let there be perfect union between us and the Giver of grace and peace. Yield all rebellion and enmity to Him, and "have peace with God through our Lord Jesus Christ"—"the peace of God,

which passeth all understanding." "And the work of righteousness shall be peace; and the effect of righteousness, quietness and confidence forever."

II. God's Purpose

1. God's Plan Before Sin Entered. Verses 3-6.

"Blessed be the God [1] and Father of our Lord Jesus Christ, who hath blessed us [2] with every spiritual blessing in the heavenly places in Christ: even as He chose us [3] in Him before the foundation of the world, that we should be holy and without blemish [4] before Him, in love: having foreordained us [5] unto adoption as sons [6] through Jesus Christ unto Himself, [7] according to the good pleasure of His will, to the praise of the glory of His grace, which He freely bestowed [8] on us in the Beloved."

NOTE AND COMMENT

1. **"Blessed be the God."**—The margin reads, "Blessed be God and the Father of our Lord Jesus Christ." The text seems to be clearer,—"Blessed be the God and Father of our Lord Jesus Christ." The word "blessed" is used in the sense of praise. All praise to Him. He is the Giver of all good, the Creator of all things, the Upholder of the universe, a marvelous, everlasting provider. Surely every child of His ought to join with the apostle in ascribing to Him blessing. This expression is one of the seven which John uses in Revelation 5:12, as belonging also to the Lamb.

2. **"Who hath blessed us."**— The expression is comprehensive. He would have us understand that God's blessing includes all. It is not limited to one thing; it includes every blessing,— not only the blessings of the earthly, but the blessings of the heavenly.

Earth of itself furnishes no blessings. In its perverted, sin-cursed state, it brings curses. "Cursed is the ground for thy sake," was the word to our first father; but out of the heavenlies in Christ, God has brought down all the blessings and bestowed them upon His children. To this he refers again, as we shall find in our study of the book.

But take note of this, and do not put the spiritual blessings far off in the uncertain future: He "hath blessed us." The blessings are ours now, even as Christ is given now. "For in Him dwelleth all the fullness of the Godhead bodily, and in

Him ye are made full." Col. 2:9, 10. He would have our faith grasp these now. The tense of the verbs is present. He has exalted us by the gift of His Son, who died in our behalf, and who Himself was made one of the human family, to a seat in the heavenly places. He would have us occupy it. He would not have us insult the royal Giver by refusing to take it because we are unworthy. He would have us believe the royal promise, and in the worthiness of our Lord sit with Him together in the heavenly places. Eph. 2:6.

How such a conception would take away all of our timidity in the world! How it would give us boldness to meet all the world's scoffs and jeers and sneers! How it would enable us to meet all the trials and conflicts and seeming darkness of life, to know that in it all we were with Christ, we were with Him also in the heavenly places! It is one of the divine and blessed paradoxes of Scripture that, while we are here, He the Heavenly One is with us, and while He, our Brother beloved in the flesh, is there, we are there with Him. But remember that as was Abraham we are blessed that we may pass on the blessings.

3. "Even as He chose us."— It is not a separating out of individual cases, choosing some "to heaven and some to hell, all for His glory." That is not a part of God's choosing. God chose character in the very beginning, a certain number of a certain character, to completely fill the home of this earth which He had provided for them. See Gen. 1:26; Ps. 115:16; Isa. 45:17, 18. The names of these characters were written in the Lamb's book of life from before the foundation of the world (Rev. 17:8); and when God calls us, He calls us to one of the chosen names, and counts that name ours when we begin the Christian life (Phil. 4:3). The name of that character shall never be blotted out. That "crown of life," "crown of righteousness," "crown of glory" (James 1:12; 2 Tim. 4:8; 1 Peter 5:4) that awaits the conqueror, will never fade or wither. That inheritance to which the soul is called, shall never pass away; and when God calls one of the children of earth, as He calls every one to one of those characters, His calling is "without repentance." The failure will always be on our part, not His; and every spiritual blessing in heavenly places in Christ will be bestowed upon that soul, that he may reach that character. And so by choosing us to one of those eternal characters, which were in God's plan before the foundation of the world, God has chosen us before the foundation of the world in that character to which He calls. And the trials and conflicts and perplexities and struggles and triumphs of this life are the putting away of the wrong education which the world has given us, are the development of a right character in His sight, are the spelling out, letter by letter, of the new name which shall be wholly ours when the overcoming is complete. Rev. 3 : 5, 12.

4. **"Holy and without blemish."**— The one thing of worth in the entire universe of God is character. The only thing which will endure throughout all eternity is character. The only thing that makes our God the worthy Being that He is, is character. Men may be worth their millions, may own and rule the world, may pile their wealth mountain-high, and their fame may be world-wide, but it is all of no worth without character. When they die all is left, and all the things that men may gather in this life will not tunnel the grave; but character does, and it is to character that God chooses His children; and those who in Him (for it is in Christ that we are chosen before the foundation of the world) gain that glorious character shall have all the riches of God's universe throughout all eternity. "Holy and without blemish" before Him, in His presence they shall verify in their own lives the song of the psalmist, "In Thy presence is fullness of joy; in Thy right hand there are pleasures forevermore." Let us take home to our hearts the blessed lesson.

5. **"Having in love foreordained us."**— We have taken the marginal reading of the last of verse 4 and the first of verse 5. It is true that we should be holy and without blemish before Him in love, but it seems to us that it is more necessary of emphasis to say, as the margin reads, that "in love" He has "foreordained us." "Predestinated" reads the common version; "marked out beforehand." It has been with no hate, or indifference even, that God has marked out, or predestinated, His children. God is love, and all that He has wrought for us, or marked out for us, or marked us out for, has been in love.

"Never careless hand, and vain,
Smites these chords of joy and pain;
No immortal selfishness
Plays the game of curse and bless:
Heaven and earth are witnesses
That Thy glory goodness is."

6. "Unto adoption as sons."— This tells us the object of His love. It gives the lie to the old black theology, born in the despair of heathenism, that God foreordained men to destruction. His foreordination takes in only that which is good; His call, His invitation, is broad enough to include every soul who will; and those who will not, take themselves out of God's great plan. God foreordained, predestinated, marked us out, to be sons of the Most High. There can be no higher call, no greater station, and it is eternal. How gladly ought men to submit to such a foreordination as that to which He calls every soul who is capable of responding to a call.

7. "Through Jesus Christ unto Himself."— We have the channel, or agent; we have the ultimate object. The ultimate object of His foreordination is to bring us "unto Himself;" children "unto Himself" in character, in holiness, without blemish; "unto Himself" "in love;" "unto Himself" in the giving out of that love to all around us on every side. We could not be God's children and be selfish. We can not be the effectual recipients of His love without giving that love in return. In other words, we can not receive that love into our lives without bestowing love upon others, and love does not diminish by the giving; it grows in its bestowing. And Jesus Christ, the eternal Word, is the One through whom the Father gathers to Himself the children of earth. It is not Father against Son, nor Son against Father, it is both working together for the good of earth's children.

8. "Freely bestowed."— God's grace is not something which is doled out stingily; it is not something which we must buy by wealth, or toil, or sacrifice. It does not demand that we should walk hundreds of miles on our hands and blistered and bleeding knees, nor that we should lie for days or weeks upon numerous spikes, or wear hair shirts, or torture ourselves in a thousand imaginable ways. God's grace is not so purchased.

It comes to us because God is love, and it comes freely. He freely bestows it, sinner. We may say that we are unworthy; we are. It is not our unworthiness that moves Him to give us His love; it is our great need. Phil. 4:19. He sees the possibility through His grace of what we may be, and He freely bestows it, bestows it even while we are in sin, in order that He may win us to Himself; and when that time comes that the heart is won, He bestows it even more abundantly, that the old life of sin may be cleansed away, and His own character, "holy and without blemish," may shine out in us.

2. After Sin Entered. Verses 7-12.

"In whom we have our redemption [1] through His blood,[2] the forgiveness of our trespasses,[3] according to the riches of His grace,[4] which He made to abound [5] toward us in all wisdom and prudence, making known [6] unto us the mystery of His will,[7] according to His good pleasure [8] which He purposed in Him [9] unto a dispensation of the fullness of the times, to sum up all things [10] in Christ, the things in the heavens, and the things upon the earth; in Him, I say, in whom also we were made a heritage,[11] having been foreordained [12] according to the purpose [13] of Him who worketh [14] all things [15] after the counsel of His will; to the end that we should be unto the praise of His glory,[16] we who had before hoped in Christ." [17]

NOTE AND COMMENT

1. **"In whom we have our redemption."**— Man can not buy himself. No combination of men can buy another back from the sin into which men have fallen. It is not a matter of purchase. Sin is a disease, a deadly disease,— mortal, fatal, always, so far as the human heart is concerned. It was the contemplation of this which led the prophet to exclaim, "The heart is deceitful above all things, and it is desperately sick." Jer. 17:9, R. V. The American Revised puts it, "and it is exceedingly corrupt;" the Common Version, "and desperately wicked." Paul very gently puts it, in Romans 3:23, as coming "short of the glory of God." But in the seventh chapter of Romans, he likens it to a body of death, with which the poor, sinful soul must be weighted until he himself is overcome with it, and which led him to exclaim, "O wretched man that I am! who shall deliver me from the body of this death?" Rom. 7:24, A. V. Truly the psalmist sang, in speaking of mortals,

"None of them can by any means redeem his brother, nor give to God a ransom for him." Ps. 49:7. But God in His mercy gave His only-beloved Son, and that Son in love gave Himself. John 3:16; Titus 2:14. The price paid was an infinite one: He died to redeem us. In Him we have our redemption, slaves bought back from the bondage of sin; and all, irrespective of age, or race, or tribe, or nation, or sex, belong to Him by purchase.

2. **"Through His blood."**— The blood stands for the life. Lev. 17:11. The life of the flesh is the blood. Jesus was "the Word made flesh." We can not understand, we need not to understand, all the mysteries of it; faith can grasp the great fact. "When the fullness of the time came, God sent forth His Son, born of a woman, born under the law, that He might redeem them that were under the law, that we might receive the adoption of sons." Gal. 4:4. "He poured out His soul unto death;" and in the last expiring agonies of the cross Heaven itself seemed shut out from Him, as He bore the penalty of even the impenitent. Had it not been for the perfect, righteous character, free from every stain of sin, the Son of God would not have come back from the grave. But it had no power over Him (Acts 2:24), because there was no sin upon Him of His own; yet He bore our sins, for "Him who knew no sin [God] made to be sin on our behalf; that we might become the righteousness of God in Him." 2 Cor. 5:21. We are redeemed by the precious blood of Christ. 1 Peter 1:19.

3. **"The forgiveness of our trespasses."**— What a blessed thing the forgiveness of sins is to one who hates sin! How even the hardened heart of the sinner at times, wooed by the blessed Spirit of God, longs to be free from sin. He looks back over a dark past; he sees where he has wronged others, more than all else, wronged his own soul, turned from his Maker and Saviour. Sometimes his crime haunts him. He goes over it again in his dreams. If he believes God, he knows that sometime it will face him in the judgment; it has eaten out the very moral fiber of his life. Truly, it is a body of death which drags down to destruction; and its deadly contagion breeds death in the sinner. James 1:15. But there is forgiveness, and forgiveness of our trespasses means that the tres-

passes are forgiven,—taken away, so that God looks upon us as sinless in His sight. The righteousness of God in Christ Jesus is imputed to us for our sinfulness; it is the changing of the old, filthy garment of our own failures for that woven in the loom of heaven by Christ Jesus our Lord. Read the graphic picture told in Isaiah 61: "I will greatly rejoice in Jehovah, my soul shall be joyful in my God; for He hath clothed me with the garments of salvation, He hath covered me with the robe of righteousness, as a bridegroom decketh himself with a garland, and as a bride adorneth herself with her jewels." Verse 10. See also verse 3.

4. **"According to the riches of His grace."**— How good it is that God does not work according to our poor, mean conceptions of His goodness! He does not forgive us as men forgive. He does not say, I will forgive you if you will never sin again. He freely forgives. Even though He knows that we may sin the next day, yet He freely forgives if we are truly repentant. He knows, whether we see the possibility of failure in our heart or not; but He sees, He knows, that we may fail to-morrow. We do not know it, and the tender, penitent heart does not feel that it will; but God knows it, knows that we are children, knows that He can not teach us so that we could appreciate that we would stumble again. But He forgives, and forgives us in order that we may know that there is no being in all the universe that welcomes us back from the fall, who is so ready to reach out the divine helping hand and lift us up, as is He.

The permanent turning away of mortals from God is not because God will not forgive; it is because the human heart becomes so saturated with sin that it will not return to God. Praise God, He forgives "according to the riches of His grace," so that inspired prayer left us through the psalmist after he had committed his awful sin, opens with these words of encouragement to the sinner: "Have mercy upon me, O God, according to Thy loving-kindness: according to the multitude of Thy tender mercies blot out my transgressions." Ps. 51:1. It is the prayer for the sinner to plead. God has left it on record; and every prayer that He has left on record His Spirit waits to "make good" to the one who will appropriate it by faith; so He grants us forgiveness "according to the riches of

His grace," the eternal riches in Christ Jesus. And then He looks upon us as though we had never sinned.

5. "Made to abound."—Always to abound, all that is necessary; and yet He gives grace in "wisdom and prudence;" but the wisdom and prudence is such that there is never a lack. When men try to draw the line of prudence, sometimes it makes them niggardly and stingy; not so with God. The grace abounds above the sin, for "where sin abounded, grace did abound more exceedingly." "Exceeding abundantly above all that we ask or think." Jehovah is the God, "abundant in loving-kindness and truth." Rom. 5:20. "Mercy glorieth against judgment." He does not give us too much. There are some whom Satan would encourage to be very great; they want not only forgiveness of sins, but they want recognition as great men in God's cause. So far as the development of workers is concerned, God tests men in all wisdom and prudence. There is always-abounding grace for the forgiveness of sins; there is always prudent grace in the development of our own soul for service. Let us be willing to leave it all with Him,— grace for forgiveness of sin, grace for victory over sin, and all the grace that we need to serve Him where He chooses.

6. "Making known."— Our God is not a being who withholds Himself from His children. He is the great Revealer. He so stands forth as against all the false gods. The gods of old time veiled their meaning in equivocal, hidden sayings or riddles. We read in the second chapter of Daniel that, unlike the gods of the Chaldeans, Jehovah revealed Himself to His children. He reveals Himself in His works,—"The heavens declare the glory of God; and the firmament showeth His handiwork." Ps. 19:1. He reveals Himself in His word,—"The secret things belong unto Jehovah our God; but the things that are revealed belong unto us and to our children forever." Deut. 29:29. God's Book is the disclosure in words of the wonderful goodness of God. These things are always revealed for our good. God also reveals the future: "He revealeth the deep and secret things; He knoweth what is in the darkness, and the light dwelleth with Him." Dan. 2:22. "There is a God in heaven that revealeth secrets, and He hath made known . . . what shall be in the latter days." Verse 28. He presents before us as a characteristic of His Godhead His power to reveal the future: "I am God, and there is none like Me; declaring the end from the beginning, and from ancient times things that are not yet done." Isa. 46:9, 10. "Surely the Lord Jehovah will do nothing, except He reveal His secret unto His servants the prophets." Amos 3:7.

But our text implies more than this. He makes known unto us "the mystery of His will." "Mystery" is one of the key words of this remarkable epistle. The heathen gods and the heathen religions had their mysteries performed in their temples, hidden from humanity, known only to the initiated; really amounting to nothing after they were known. But they were the means of holding wonderful power over the superstitious and uninitiated, but never affecting for good the life of the one who knew the mystery. Not so the mystery of God. It is a mystery, but it is free to all. All may be initiated; all may know, if all will meet God's simple conditions.

7. **"Mystery of His will."**— For "mystery," see Romans 11:25; Colossians 1:26. It is God's grace as manifested in redemption. It is the power of that grace laying hold upon the human heart. It was manifest in our Lord Jesus Christ, who was "born of a woman, born under the law." Gal. 4:4, 5. It is "the mystery of godliness" set over against "the mystery of lawlessness." 1 Tim. 3:16; 2 Thess. 2:7. To the child of faith, this mystery is solved. "The Word became flesh, and dwelt among us," that Word revealing the very character of God; and God has left us that Word which, in response to faith, will transmute poor mortal man into the divine image, "Christ in you, the hope of glory." Col. 1:27. It is we yielding all to Him, and He, Redeemer, Saviour, Sanctifier, coming into our life and making us "to the praise of the glory of His grace." It is what the apostle means elsewhere by "sanctification;" and so we read, "For this is the will of God, even your sanctification." 1 Thess. 4:3. God, then, has made known the mystery of His will in order that we may be re-created and changed after His own character, in harmony with His own will.

8. **"According to His good pleasure."**—God is good, and His ways are always good. He who is love can do no otherwise

than good. That is not saying that our condition might not
be greatly bettered; but God is doing just as well for us as it
is possible for Him to do. If we stood nearer to Him, our
hearts more in harmony with His blessed will, He would be
able to do larger things for us; but all that He does is to do
us good, yet not always, it seems to us, in the very present
time. The seed sowing means the breaking of the ground,
means the rain, and means the harrow, means all the hard
things that come upon the ground; but it also means fruitage
as well.

We therefore read of the Lord's purpose concerning Israel
of old: "Who led thee through the great and terrible wilderness, wherein were fiery serpents and scorpions, and thirsty
ground, where there was no water; who brought thee forth
water out of the rock of flint; who fed thee in the wilderness
with manna, which thy fathers knew not; that He might
humble thee, and that He might prove thee, to do *thee good at
thy latter end.*" Deut. 8:15, 16. The "terrible wilderness,"
the "fiery serpents," the "scorpions," the "thirsty ground,"
did not seem good; but God had in mind the greater good
which would accrue from the enduring of all these. And therefore we read again His words to backsliding Israel: "For I
know the thoughts that I think toward you, saith Jehovah,
thoughts of peace, and not of evil, to give you hope in your latter
end," or, as the margin reads, "a latter end and hope." Jer. 29:11.

It is the good pleasure of our God to save men. It is not
God's pleasure to destroy men. It is sin that destroys, not
God. He·Himself emphasizes this as strongly as language
can: "Say unto them, As I live, saith the Lord Jehovah, I have
no pleasure in the death of the wicked; but that the wicked
turn from his way and live: turn ye, turn ye from your evil
ways; for why will ye die?" Eze. 33:11. It was God's pleasure, therefore, to have mercy. Pleasure is delight; and thus
He declares to His children: "Jehovah taketh pleasure in them
that fear Him, in those that hope in His mercy." Ps. 147:11.
Well may we say, "Who is a God like unto Thee, that par-
doneth iniquity, and passeth over the transgression of the
remnant of His heritage? He retaineth not His anger forever,
because He delighteth in loving-kindness. He will again have

compassion upon us; He will tread our iniquities underfoot; and Thou wilt cast all their sins into the depths of the sea." Micah 7:18, 19. Even so God has made known the mystery of His will "according to His good pleasure."

9. **"Which He purposed in Him;"** that is, in Himself. "The reference is clearly to God," says Vincent, not to Christ, who is expressly mentioned in the next verse. How good to know that the purpose is in One who is able to perform it, the eternal Jehovah! In union with that purpose, we are safe. In union with that purpose, it is God's good pleasure to do for us all that the purpose embraces.

10. **"To sum up all things."**—"Unto a dispensation of the fullness of the times," or unto the dispensation,—"the mystery . . . which He purposed in Him unto a dispensation." The word "dispensation" comes from *oikos,* a house; and *nemo,* to dispense, or manage. A dispensation is the work of a house steward in the managing of his house,—a stewardship. God's purpose is wrought through our Lord Jesus Christ, who is working out in the house of God all God's plans. "But Christ as a Son, over His own house [that is, God's house]; whose house are we, if we hold fast our boldness and the glorying of our hope firm unto the end." Heb. 3:6. But this steward-ship, or dispensation, of our Lord looks forward·to the fullness of the times, to the completion of all the travail of sin and woe and misery, past all this to the glorious ingathering of His kingdom, when God will gather together in one all things in Christ; when the great sacrifice which the universe has made of its Creator under God shall be manifest in glorious fruitage; when our Redeemer "shall see of the travail of His soul, and shall be satisfied;" and when the divisive power of sin shall be forever put away, because sin is forever banished.

11. **"Made a heritage."**— In our Common Version, it is "have obtained an inheritance." The thought seems to include both "obtained an inheritance" and "made a heritage." The Greek word *"eklērothēmen"* occurs only here in the New Testament. It comes from *klēros,* a lot. Hence the verb means literally, to determine, to choose, or to assign by lot; and Vincent tells us that from the custom of assigning portions of land by lot, *klēros* acquires the meaning of that which is thus assigned, the

possession, or portion, of land. See the Septuagint on Num-
bers 24:18; Deuteronomy 3:18. An heir is originally one who
obtains by lot. "The Authorized Version here makes the verb
active, where it should be passive. The literal sense is, we
were designated as a heritage; so the Revised Version cor-
rectly, 'were made a heritage.' Compare Deuteronomy 4:20,
'a people of inheritance.'" So God has made His people a
people of inheritance. He does not design that they should be
pilgrims and wanderers forever. This earth in its present condition is not their home. Moses tells us: "When the Most
High gave to the nations their inheritance, when He separated
the children of men, He set the bounds of the peoples according to the number of the children of Israel. For Jehovah's
portion is His people; Jacob is the lot of His inheritance."
Deut. 32:8, 9. But this does not pertain to this earth alone,
and its present divisions, political and otherwise.

"The earth is Jehovah's, and the fullness thereof;" and
when God's purpose is complete, "the meek shall inherit the
earth." "From sea to sea," and "from the River unto the ends
of the earth," God's children will have their habitation; and
in God's design every one of His children shall there have
inheritance. To that He has called them; for that He has
made them "a people of inheritance." The bounds of the
peoples then, and the number of the children of Israel then,
will be such as to fill completely the new heavens and the new
earth, which will be given to them.

All that brings disunion in this world, into God's kingdom
anywhere, is sin. All the perversion of human reason, of fac-
ulties, of judgment, of moral conduct, of anything and everything evil, is because of sin. Sin will be put away; and the
great summing up will take place, predicted in Revelation
5:13: "And every created thing which is in the heaven, and
on the earth, and under the earth, and on the sea, and all things
that are in them, heard I saying, Unto Him that sitteth on the
throne, and unto the Lamb, be the blessing, and the honor, and
the glory, and the dominion forever and ever." All heaven and
earth are then united; the unity of God's creation restored.
Earth is no more a lost island, separated from the continent
of heaven by a gulf of sin; nay, it has not been separated even

in its sin, for the love of Christ has bridged it. But the love of Christ and all His creatures will bridge it in that glorious new day when all God's children shall be one, and all His universe one, and one life will throb through it all from the great heart of Heaven. And all this is found in "the good pleasure of His will."

12. **"Having been foreordained."**—"Predestinated," Common Version; literally, "foremarked out, or limited." The thought of the apostle all the way through is not on the negative side of the great question. He is not presenting before us the doom of the impenitent, or of the incorrigibly wicked. What he is setting before us is God's purpose concerning His children. Let us bear in mind that nowhere is it said that God has foreordained us to destruction. Hold the assurance of the apostle, "For God appointed us not unto wrath, but unto the obtaining of salvation through our Lord Jesus Christ." 1 Thess. 5:9.

13. **"According to the purpose."**— God has a purpose in all that He does. Man works purposelessly many times. That is the whole tendency of sin, to make purposeless the best purposes of humanity, and oh, how many times sin succeeds! Man has noble purposes which he endeavors to carry out for himself and in himself and by himself, but they fail. There is one purpose, however, which will be carried out, and that is God's great purpose concerning man and man's heritage and man's future. We briefly note it:

First, the earth was created for the children of men. God gave His command in the beginning that men should multiply and completely fill the earth. This we learn in Genesis 1. In Isaiah 45:17, 18, God has made oath by Himself that it is not created in vain; it is formed to be inhabited. And He assures us that that purpose will be carried out, by the thought, "I am Jehovah; and there is none else." He must, in His perfect purpose, design that the earth should be inhabited by a certain number of a certain character. "Behold, . . . God made man upright" (Eccl. 7:29), said the wise man; He formed man in His own image, we learn in the original account (Gen. 1:27).

There should, therefore, be a certain number of a certain character to inhabit the earth,— not too many, or it would be crowded, and some one would lack inheritance; not too few, or there would be barrenness and lonesomeness and vacancy. Not only nature, but God, abhors a vacuum; there could therefore be no unused spaces. Every one of God's children shall have inheritance, or lot, in that earth as it came from God's hand "very good." But sin came in and marred God's handiwork, and God's children, instead of inheriting the earth, have oftentimes been the persecuted ones, and those that have been deprived not only of a portion of earth, but of life as well; they have been pilgrims and strangers. Nevertheless, the purpose stands.

We may also readily believe, as intimated elsewhere in His Word, that the names of those characters which would inherit the earth, were written in God's long roll of life before the world was made. The perfect purpose demanded it. These characters would be overcomers, and there were crowns that should await the character, and they still wait—the crown, the name, the character—for those of earth who shall meet the conditions. When once a soul yields to the Lord Jesus, his own name is written in the book of life. Phil. 4:3. His own name is written there as a candidate for the name of the everlasting character, written there in the beginning, before mankind was. The crown that is suitable to that name awaits the overcomer; but if he fails, his own name will be blotted out of the book of life. Rev. 3:5. He will fail to receive his crown. Rev. 3:11. But the name of the character will remain, and the crown will remain, and the inheritance will remain for some one else that will be called to that name and that crown and that character; for God's eternal purpose concerning the earth and man and character will not fail.

14. **"Who worketh."**— All the infinite power of the Creator is behind His call to the sinner. The potency of that call is the potency of perfect character to him who will yield to it, and hope in Jesus Christ. It may seem to be impossible to us —utterly so—having tested our own disposition, having known something of its weaknesses, its utter unholiness and unlikeness to God. How many times we were prepared to listen to the discouraging doubts of the enemy that there is no hope in God for us! but we trust in a Being of all power. He who can take the insensate earth and form it into the

marvel of the rose, who can, from the slimy, stagnant pool, bring all the beauty and purity and fragrance of the lily, can take poor mortals of earth and make them "to the praise of His glory."

15. "Who worketh all things."— How good it is to know that the One who has formed the purpose, who has marked out the character, who in the beginning made the earth, is able to do all that He purposes to do! He "worketh all things"—not after the counsel of human will, not after the perversion of that will by demons or men, but—"after the counsel of His will." Despite all the perversions of sin, God's will will be wrought out. It looks otherwise sometimes. It seems as though the accusations of "the accuser of our brethren" were true. It seems as though God had Himself become a tyrant, and so Satan makes men believe. It seems as though He were weak, or unable to carry out His will, as though all His purposes were thwarted, as though He had forgotten humanity.

But all these things are in the seeming. God remembers, God cares; for God is love. And so in love, though our short-sightedness may not see it, He is working out all things after the counsel of His will. Man may fail, God will not fail. Satan may seem to thwart His purposes, but out of the conflict His purposes will come all the more glorious. When the devotees of the gods of Egypt seemed to triumph, Jehovah was above them; and in the great final triumph it will be seen that He is preëminently, gloriously, Conqueror, and all those who are with Him are triumphant. He can not arbitrarily set aside the sinner; He can not arbitrarily in His plan overthrow the one who commits the sin in its inception,—that would seem many times to be acting unjustly. He must let sin work out its own essential evils. He must let it bear its crop of fearful fruit, in order that the universe may see in the object lessons how exceedingly sinful sin is.

16. "The praise of His glory."— We have seen unsightly piles of stone and brick and sand, barrels of cement and lime, timbers of various lengths and sizes, by the side of a pleasant street, covering the walk. The way is obstructed, street and walk are well covered with dirt. It is an unseemly mass. Soon trenches are dug, and conditions look worse. But men come,— architect, builder, workmen. We leave the town for a few days, and return to find on the spot a noble palace, symmetrical and beautiful. Who is the architect and designer? Mr. Ward. Who is the builder? Mr. Herndon. And as you and others view the palace inside and out, the praises of architect and designer are sung.

God takes wrecks of men and women,— marred, warped, blasted, blighted by sin, hopeless in themselves; but if they yield to Him "who worketh all things after the counsel of His will," by His creative power and abounding grace He reconstructs and makes "unto the praise of His glory" these souls wrecked by Satan and sin. Throughout all eternity they will show forth His praise in the beauty and glory of characters immortal.

17. "We who had [margin, have] before hoped in Christ." —We who have yielded ourselves as candidates for the name, the crown, the inheritance. It matters not what we are; it matters not who we are, when God calls us. We may be such as those of whom He speaks in 1 Corinthians 6:9,—fornicators, idolaters, adulterers, effeminate, abusers of themselves with men, thieves, covetous, drunkards, revilers, extortioners. We are there told that such shall not inherit the kingdom of God; but we are also told that such were some of the Corinthian brethren. They once belonged to these classes; "but ye were justified in the name of the Lord Jesus Christ, and in the Spirit of our God."

This lesson in Ephesians is a message for you, discouraged soul, whoever you are. Satan may have overcome you. You may have sinned. You may be discouraged in the progress that you are making. Turn away from all these discouragements. Yield yourself to His will and to the workings of the power of His Spirit. He will enable you day by day to spell out the letters in that new name. Win victories to-day that will entitle you to be the wearer of the crown, and help you by His grace and power to share some part of that glorious inheritance that awaits the victor. Yield all to Him, accept all from Him. Your hope is not in princes; it is not in what humanity can do; it is what God in Christ has already done for you. Then hope on, hope ever. He is able to do "exceeding abundantly" above all that you ask or think.

3. Word of Truth and Holy Spirit, Verses 13, 14.

"In whom [1] ye also, having heard the word of the truth, the gospel of your salvation,— in whom, having also believed,[2] ye were sealed with the Holy Spirit of promise,[3] which is an earnest of our inheritance,[4] unto the redemption of God's own possession,[5] unto the praise of His glory." [6]

NOTE AND COMMENT

1. "In whom"— that is, in Christ. The participial clause in the beginning of the verse brings in a thought which is worthy of our note,—"in whom . . . having heard the word of the truth;" and "the word of the truth" he declares to be "the gospel of your salvation." That is what the positive side of God's truth always is to His children. We read in Psalm 119: 142, "Thy righteousness is an everlasting righteousness, and Thy law is truth." But all God's truth is not comprehended in His law as such. Our text declares that the gospel is truth. All the great positive, living facts of God's word are truth.

The truth differs from fact in this, that facts are mere dead things, statements of things that are so, or have been so; but truth is always living, and God's truth throbs with His life. The psalmist has expressed it: "The sum of Thy Word is truth." It includes both God's law and His gospel. The law reveals to us sin; the gospel takes away the sin and writes in our hearts the holy law, so that it no longer condemns us, but becomes a witness of the righteousness which we receive though the gospel. Therefore Paul was not ashamed of the gospel of Christ, because that in it was revealed the righteousness of God. Rom. 1:16. But the word is living truth only as it is received in Him — in whom ye heard. He before said, "The words that I have spoken unto you are spirit, and are life." John 6:63.

2. "In whom, having also believed."— Bible belief, or living belief, is not mere assent to a proposition. There are thousands who assent to facts; that is not Bible belief. The belief which is effective is that which brings living union with Christ.

The apostle has expressed it in another place thus: "With the heart man believeth unto righteousness." It does not stop short of appropriating the righteousness which God gives us through Jesus Christ. It does not stop short of the righteousness which He wishes developed in our lives. It does not stop short of a faithful, dutiful, commandment-keeping heart, a heart that could say with the psalmist, "Oh how love I Thy law! It is my meditation all the day" (Ps. 119:97); or with "the beloved disciple," "For this is the love of God, that we keep His commandments: and His commandments are not grievous" (1 John 5:3). Such is true Bible belief, such is the fruitage of faith.

3. **"Ye were sealed with the Holy Spirit of promise."**— Belief brings the Spirit of God. In fact, it is the Spirit of God that is the operating power of the Most High in every process of conversion and regeneration. It is the Spirit of God that broods over the sinner as it did over the waste of darkness in the beginning. Gen. 1:2. It is the Spirit that presses home upon the sinner the fact that he is a sinner, that enables him to see himself as God's law reveals him, which presses upon his heart, as it did upon the heart of the apostle Paul, that "the law is spiritual: but I am carnal, sold under sin." It is the Spirit that brings to his mind the word of the gospel, that there is hope in the Lord Jesus Christ. And, finally, it is that Spirit that writes upon his heart God's law, and thus seals the soul as one of the family of God. It gives assurance to the child of God, because it changes his heart from hatred of God's law to love of God's law. "Old things are passed away; behold they are become new."

He does not then see the law as an avenging sword hung over his head, but as a blessed guide, a monitor; and the Spirit writing that law within his heart brings him the twofold witness of the law without and the law within, revealing to him that he is truly a child of God. And thus the Word gives two-fold witness: "The Spirit Himself beareth witness with our spirit, that we are children of God: and if children, then heirs; heirs of God, and joint heirs with Christ."

A seal is that which makes an impression, or stamp. It is used in official documents as a testimony that the one who sealed it has acknowledged and legalized the document to which it is attached. So it is that God stamps those children who yield themselves to Him as His own, placing upon them His own character. The Holy Spirit is the Sealer, not the seal,

4. **"Earnest of our inheritance."**—"Earnest" means pledge. It is a not uncommon thing for men to pay earnest, or pledge, money; for instance, a drover purchases cattle of the farmers and does not pay all the price until the cattle are delivered on a certain day; but he pays a portion of that money to bind the bargain. That is earnest money. It binds both parties: it binds the drover to take the cattle and pay the rest of the money on a stipulated day when the farmer delivers them, and it also binds the farmer to hold those cattle for the drover, and prevents his selling them to anyone else. It is, in fact, a part payment, sometimes called "caution money." It is a deposit in pledge of full payment. So God gives His Holy Spirit to His children as a pledge of the glorious immortality at His coming.

5. **"Unto the redemption of God's own possession."**— The word "possession" means preservation, preservation for one's self; acquisition; a thing acquired, or a possession; used here collectively for the people possessed. "God's own possession," in the Revised Version, is simply an insertion of "God's own" for the sake of clearness. (See Vincent's "Word Studies.") So the "earnest" money of God — the Holy Spirit — is given to His children to assure them that they are God's own possession, and that the inheritance, the glorious immortality which lies before, will be theirs. Trouble may intervene; God remains the same. Death may cut one off temporarily; but the inheritance waits. And the One who has given the Spirit, and has promised the inheritance, has broken the power of the grave, and will bring all His children home. They are His own possession. He counts them, though their graves number millions, as still alive, because, in His purpose, they are alive, and will live when the Lord Jesus shall come the second time.

> "God's ways seem dark, but soon or late
> They touch the shining hills of day.
> The evil can not brook delay.
> The good can well afford to wait."

6. **"Unto the praise of His glory."**— Three times we have this expression, almost in the same words: the first in its application to God's plan (verses 3-6),—"to the praise of the glory of His grace;" the second in the working out of that plan despite of sin,—"unto the praise of His glory;" and the third the development of character in each individual by the power of the Spirit,—"unto the praise of His glory." So it all shall be. All the efforts of the enemy of all righteousness to thwart God's plan shall in the end redound to His glory. That is His purpose that He has predestinated. He invites all to fall in with His purpose, the pleasure of His will. He has not predestinated death; He has predestinated character and life. If we will yield to His word, the character will be ours, the inheritance ours, the consummation of the work of the Spirit ours; and we shall be "to the praise of the glory of His grace" throughout all eternity. Thus ends the longest and greatest sentence in the Bible.

III. A God-Breathed Prayer for the Church. Verses 15-23.

"For this cause[1] I also, having heard of the faith in the Lord Jesus which is among you, and the love which ye show toward all the saints, cease not to give thanks[2] for you, making mention of you in my prayers; that the God of our Lord Jesus Christ, the Father of glory, may give[3] unto you a spirit of wisdom and revelation in the knowledge of Him; having the eyes of your heart enlightened,[4] that ye may know[5] what is the hope of His calling, what the riches of the glory of His inheritance in the saints, and what the exceeding greatness of His power[6] to usward who believe, according to that working of the strength of His might which He wrought in Christ, when He raised Him from the dead, and made Him to sit[7] at His right hand in the heavenly places, far above all rule,[8] and authority, and power, and dominion, and every name that is named, not only in this world,[9] but also in that which is to come, and He put all things in subjection[10] under His feet, and gave Him to be head over all things to the church,[11] which is His body,[12] the fullness of Him that filleth all in all."

NOTE AND COMMENT

1. **"For this cause."**— That is, that God had wrought out His wonderful purpose, and by His Spirit made effective this purpose in the hearts of all His believing children; and the apostle had heard that this faith was in the Ephesian brethren. It was manifest among them, or, as the margin reads, "in them." It

was personal faith on their part, uniting them with the Lord
Jesus Christ; it lead them to love with the same affection with
which Christ loved. They not only had faith in Him, but Paul
had heard also of the love which they showed toward all the
saints. The strongest bond of union between God's children is
Christ Jesus. All earthly bonds are but as tow in the flame. If
personal ambition stands in the way of mere earthly love, the
earthly love is sacrificed to personal ambition, and love turns
to hatred. But when the love is the love which is begotten by
the life of the Lord Jesus, and when He becomes the bond
between the regenerated soul and all others, the love abides;
and this was the love that was in these Christians whom Paul
is addressing.

2. **"Cease not to give thanks."**— That always ought to be
the first desideratum in prayer,— thanksgiving. Come to God
with a spirit of thanksgiving. It opens our heart toward Him,
it takes away the gloom which the enemy would bring. Think
of God's mercies, ponder His goodness, dwell upon the blessings which He is bestowing upon us, and that will give us
courage to pray. And so Paul, thanking God for these con-
verts to Christ, has courage in pleading with God for them.

3. **"That the God of our Lord Jesus Christ . . . may give."**
— He does not beat about the bush. There is no circumlocu-
tion in what He wants. He prays to the One who had made
Jesus Christ all that He is,— to the Father of glory, the One
in whom is infinite perfection and infinite fullness, the One
who has all the eternal and infinite supplies of grace and
power. He is the One whom he asks to give; and he prays,
first of all, for a spirit of wisdom and revelation in the knowledge of God. The knowledge of Jehovah, of His character, is
more than all the wisdom and power and riches that this world
can give. Jer. 9:23, 24. Of what use is it for us to seek Him
if we do not believe that He is all that He professes to be?
Paul did not want the church to be limited in knowledge. He
wanted God's Spirit (see Isa. 11:2), which is a Spirit of Wisdom and Understanding, a Spirit of Counsel and Might, a
Spirit of Knowledge and of the Fear of the Lord to give them
clear vision of what God is, the wisdom and the revelation in
the knowledge of Him.

4. **"Having the eyes of your heart enlightened."**— The world would not put it that way. It would want the mind enlightened, the intellect enlarged, scientific knowledge obtained. Many reformers plead for the enlightening of the world, and hope that reform will come through enlightenment; but it has been demonstrated repeatedly that knowledge alone increases the power to sin,—"knowledge puffeth up." There is something better than that; for "love buildeth up," and the heart is the seat of love, the seat of the affections. It here stands for that, and God wishes the heart, the affections, enlightened. Connect this with the wisdom and revelation before. He would have us have wise affections, and wise affections in our Lord Jesus Christ; and true, wise love for Him.

Humanity is led by affection and emotion and impulse more than by knowledge and reason and judgment. How often young people plunge into unwise marriages, led, not by wisdom, but by affection, impulse! Their own best judgment often questions the step, but the unwise heart controls; and the fruitage of unhappiness eventually follows. There can be no true union between a Christian and a worldling. The great jazz world throws reason and righteousness and wisdom and good counsel to the winds, and follows the way of the unenlightened, uncontrolled heart — the affections, emotions, desires. God wants the heart. "The eyes of Jehovah run to and fro throughout the whole earth, to show Himself strong in behalf of them whose heart is perfect toward Him." 2 Chron. 16:9. Therefore, "Son, give Me thine heart." Therefore first, "Thou shalt love the Lord thy God with all thy heart." Therefore, "Keep thy heart above all that thou guardest; for out of it are the issues of life." Prov. 4:23, margin. All may not have knowledge, wisdom, education, ability to speak or write, but all, thank God, may have that which is vastly superior to all, — supreme, all-dominating love to God. Let God's word guide mind and soul and heart, and the harvest will never be disappointing.

5. **"That ye may know."**—Oh, how much uncertainty there is among nominal Christians at the present time! How few really know God! They know of God, and have heard of Him;

but how few really know Him! Many have heard of hope, and they long that that hope shall be theirs, but there is no real true hope. The apostle would have them know,—"that ye may know what is the hope of His calling." That "hope of His calling" reaches through the veil, reaches beyond this life, takes hold upon the resurrection beyond. Acts 24:15. He would have them know "the hope of His calling" and "the riches of the glory of His inheritance in the saints." He would have them lay hold of all that for which Christ died, a complete salvation; He would have them possess that assurance which would claim these as their own through Him, the Master. Not through any worthiness of their own can they claim it, but in the riches of the glory of His grace. That is His purpose. It is for that Christ died. It is for that the Spirit is given. It is ours to know "the hope of His calling," and "the riches of the glory of His inheritance."

6. **"And what the exceeding greatness of His power."**— It is not the power to move the masses of the world by any arts which we possess, by any skill that we have, by any human power or prestige, but power over sin, the power which was in our Lord Jesus Christ when He was raised from the dead,— nothing short of that. But why was Christ raised from the dead? We are told in Acts 2:24 that the grave could not hold Him. Why could it not hold Him?— Because "in the way of righteousness is life; and in the pathway thereof there is no death." Prov. 12:28. The only means that the grave has of holding souls within its portals is because of the sin that is on them. Take away the sin, and they will as truly come from the grave when God calls as did our Lord Jesus Christ. The power that was in Christ was power over sin, and power over sin is power over finished sin, or death. James 1:15.

7. **"Made Him to sit."**— The power of the gospel reaches beyond this life — it gives power over sin here, but it reaches to "the heavenly places." This is the strength of God's might which He wrought in Christ, and which through Christ He would work out in every soul.

8. **"Far above all rule."**— Lucifer sought position. He aimed to take the very place of God Himself. "I will make myself

like the Most High," he said. See Isa. 14:12-14. Not so with
our Lord. When He saw man's dire need, He "emptied Himself, taking the form of a servant, being made in the likeness
of men; and being found in fashion as a man, He humbled
Himself, becoming obedient even unto death, yea, the death
of the cross." Infinite love moved Him, and therefore that
infinite love made Him worthy of the exaltation that was given
Him. "Wherefore also God highly exalted Him, and gave
Him the name which is above every name." See Phil. 2:5-9.
While in this world He was subject to authority; He was in
a physical sense given into the power of Satan, and into the
power of the authority and rule of this world. Through the
instigation of Satan, He was put to death and locked in the
rock tomb, sealed with the Roman seal; but eternal right is
eternal might: the grave could not hold Him,— God raised
Him from the dead, and exalted Him above every name that
is named.

9. **"Not only in this world."**— Literally, "not only in this
age" (see margin), not only in this time which we now see.
Sometimes Satan would lead us to doubt regarding Christ's
cause; still the Master rules, and by and by He is going to rule
fully, when all sin is put away forever in that glorious age to
come, the eternal age of the ages.

10. **"All things in subjection."**—When Jesus had arisen
from the dead, He said to His disciples, "All authority hath been
given unto Me in heaven and on earth." Matt. 28:18. Not
"all power," in the sense of energy, or might, but all "authority." It embraces more than mere energy, or strength. It is
authority to use all these. He is worthy of the authority. He
who would rule others must learn to rule himself; and our
Lord Jesus Christ won the absolute and eternal victory over
self, meeting every temptation which the enemy of souls could
devise, and coming off more than triumphant in them all.

11. **"Head over all things to the church."**— There is no
other head than Christ Jesus our Lord. Elsewhere the apostle
brings it down to an individual application: "The Head of
every man is Christ" (1 Cor. 11:3); and because the Head of
every man is Christ, the true Head of every right combination

of men is Christ. The church of Christ is not a gross material thing; its members are here upon the earth while they live, from age to age, and from generation to generation; but these members, though dwelling upon the earth, are of heavenly birth; they are born from above, and there their Head, the Lord Jesus, is. To set aside the eternal, all-embracing headship of Christ, and to put in its place an earthly head, is to usurp His authority; for He assures us not only as a church, but also as individuals, "Lo, I am with you always."

His Representative

Christ has His great Representative here, but that Representative is not a visible man, nor is it any set of men. That Representative is the Holy Spirit. "I will not leave you desolate," He tells us as He departed from us, "I come unto you." John 14:18. And then, that we may understand what He means, He says: "These things have I spoken unto you, while yet abiding with you. But the Comforter, even the Holy Spirit, whom the Father will send in My name, He shall teach you all things, and bring to your remembrance all that I said unto you." Verse 26. Again: "He [the Spirit] abideth with you, and shall be in you." Verse 17. And there are many other scriptures which state the same great truth, that the Lord Jesus Christ, the Head of the church, has but one true, divine Representative in this world with full complement of power and authority, and that is the Holy Spirit of truth.

He has other representatives, He has here His own children; but He has no vicar of Christ upon earth save the Spirit of God; and that Spirit and the teachings of that Spirit we are to know, because the teachings of that Spirit are in harmony with the Word which the Spirit has before inspired, with the law given by the voice of God at Sinai. Therefore God has given us the twofold witness of the Spirit and the Word,— the Spirit in the church and the Spirit in the Word, for the body which He has left. Christ is "Head over all things to the church," and "the Head of every man is Christ;" therefore every man can come directly to the Head without anything coming between. This does not mean that His own people will work at cross purposes. There can be no stronger bond of union between the hands and their proper coöperation than the head which guides them both; and so it is with the various members of His body.

12. "Which is His body."— The human body, the members of the human frame, are common figures with the apostle. He uses these in great detail in 1 Corinthians 12, in which he likens the various members in the church and the various gifts in the church to the various members of the body — Christ the Head, these members composing the body. The life of Christ, the thought of Christ and teaching of Christ, the obedience of Christ, to be manifest in all the actions of the body. And, too, God has made this church of His, His means of revealing the Lord Jesus to the world. Christ revealed the Father when He was upon the earth. He declares, "As the Father hath sent Me [into the world], even so send I you." Christians are to reveal Christ. They are to show forth His wisdom, His life, His character, His power.

The Lord in various ways reveals Himself to His children, sometimes by vision, sometimes by angels, always, continually, by His Word. But He does not come directly in that way to those who are outside of the church,— He reveals Himself to the outside through His church. Cornelius could be stirred by an angel to seek after God, but the Lord directs him to send for one Simon, whose surname is Peter, and he will tell him what to do. Acts 10. The apostle Paul is stricken down with conviction as to his course, and he inquires what God would have him do, and the Lord sends to him Ananias. See Acts 9.

And thus it ever is: God uses the human agent to speak to those who are without. But He does not make this human agent the lord over those who hear, or listen, or reject. Even Jesus Himself did not condemn those who did not listen, and His followers can do no more than did He. He said, "If any man hear My sayings, and keep them not, I judge him not: for I came not to judge the world, but to save the world." That is the mission of His followers, to save; and the bond between them is no arbitrary authority of church, or council, or conference, or synod, or presbytery, but the one bond of love and life in the Lord Jesus Christ, bound together for a better carrying forward of His work, and the strengthening of each other in that work. This is the object of His church militant; and in that church He has placed His wonderful graces, the fullness of Him that filleth all in all. He who recognizes that will not make of the church a deity, nor will he regard it lightly. He will find there all the imperfections of humanity, but he will also find there all the fullness of the Master, working to bring all things "to the praise of the glory of His grace."

"CHRIST designs that heaven's order, heaven's plan of government, heaven's divine harmony, shall be represented in His church on earth. Thus in His people He is glorified. Through them the Sun of Righteousness will shine in undimmed luster to the world. Christ has given to His church ample facilities, that He may receive a large revenue of glory from His redeemed, purchased possession. He has bestowed upon His people capabilities and blessings that they may represent His own sufficiency. The church, endowed with the righteousness of Christ, is His depositary, in which the riches of His mercy, His grace, and His love are to appear in full and final display. Christ looks upon His people in their purity and perfection, as the reward of His humiliation, and the supplement of His glory,— Christ, the great Center, from whom radiates all glory."—*"Desire of Ages," page 680.*

CHAPTER TWO

From Confusion to Harmony: Analysis

I. The state of the sinner by nature. Verses 1-3.
II. From death to life. Verses 4-10.
III. Things well to remember. Verses 11, 12.
IV. In Christ Jesus. Verses 13-18.
V. God's living temple. Verses 19-22.

I. Man's Condition by Nature. Verses 1-3.

"And you[1] did He make alive, when ye were dead through your trespasses and sins,[2] wherein ye once walked according to the course of this world,[3] according to the prince of the powers of the air, of the spirit that now worketh in the sons of disobedience; among whom we also all once lived[4] in the lusts of our flesh, doing the desires of the flesh and of the mind,[5] and were by nature children of wrath,[6] even as the rest."

NOTE AND COMMENT

1. **"And you."**— Let the letter of the epistle come home to each one of our hearts,— count ourselves among the "you." "You did He quicken" (A. V.), "make alive," literally. When God created man, he had the twofold life of the soul and the spirit,— the soul the life of the flesh, the life that is in the blood (Lev. 17:11), the life that is common to both man and beast; but he had a life higher than that, the spirit life, the life direct from God. Losing that, man became a dying creature; losing that, he was spiritually dead, or, as expressed by the apostle elsewhere, "separated from Christ," "without God," "alienated from the life of God," accounted dead because doomed to die, and requiring the creative power of God in order to make him alive.

2. **"Through your trespasses and sins."**— If man had lived according to the law of his being, which was the great moral law of God, he would never have died, never would have been accounted dead. The higher life was in harmony with the higher law; the lower, soulical life was in harmony with the physical law of the being. But when man transgressed the higher law of his existence, the results of that transgression extended through everything below, and the very law that

(39)

was transgressed became the power which destroyed. And so
we read in First Corinthians, "The sting of death is sin; and
the power of sin is the law," which causes the death of the
sinner. It is the turning aside of the electric current from the
wire which is supposed to be its proper channel into the body
of the man who intercepts that current, that causes his death.
He has perverted the law, or the channel, of that current's
operation. When man perverts the power of the living law of
God, that law must cause his death. All death is in conse-
quence of sin. Death is but finished sin. James 1:15. Would
we know, therefore, how evil sin is? Look upon death, its
finished work.

3. "According to the course of this world."—When man departed from God, he followed the lower plan; he chose another
leader, yielded allegiance to another kingdom, and that kingdom was the kingdom of this world, the course of this age—
this world that had yielded itself to the prince of the powers
of the air. When Lucifer transgressed the higher law of his
being, he fell, and there fell with him a third of the angels of
God. These are the powers of the air under the control of
Satan, and those who turn from God and yield to him are
walking "according to the course of this world, according to
the prince of the powers of the air, of the spirit that now worketh in the sons of disobedience."

When Adam was made the head of this world under God,
he had dominion over the fish of the sea and the fowls of the
air, over all the earth and all that pertained to it. Gen. 1:26,
28. When he yielded himself to Satan, he yielded all his
dominion, and Satan became "prince of this world" (John
12:31), "prince of the powers of the air." Hence, the fearful
destructive cyclones, tornadoes, pestilences.

4. "Among whom we also all once lived."—God makes no
discrimination among men, so far as their salvation is concerned. "All have sinned, and fall short of the glory of God."
Rom. 3:23. "There is none righteous, no, not one." All, therefore, need saving. Some have not yielded themselves to sin as
deeply as others. Some are not as sick with the awful malady
of sin as are others, but the same deadly disease germs are
indigenous to every son and daughter of Adam, and without

Christ we all follow the lusts of our flesh. There is no respect of persons with God. However men may regard them, He sees mankind utterly lost and without hope in themselves.

5. "Doing the desires of the flesh and of the mind."— The flesh is sinful flesh, and the mind is the carnal mind, or the mind of the flesh. See Rom. 8:7. The doing, therefore, is fleshly, sinful doing; in fact, there can be no other doing. One is bound to sin who is ruled by the carnal mind. Outwardly his works may seem to be good, but the motive that prompts him is a selfish motive after all. There is no difference between the purchasing power of a dollar given by a sinner and a dollar given by a righteous man. There is greater potency, however, in the latter for good than there is in the former. The one has behind it the selfish motive and selfish thought of the giver; the other has behind it a life that is consecrated to God, a prayer that the dollar may be used for all that God designed that it should be used in the conversion of souls to Him. It is not that God wishes to decry or belittle the deeds which men do, the efforts they put forth to do good; it is that He may save them that He lays bare the hopeless condition of the man without a divine Saviour.

6. "Children of wrath."— The Bible calls men the children of that which they assimilate in character. Jesus called the Jews the children of the devil, because they were doing the work that Satan would have them. Some of them are called children of Belial, or worthlessness, because of their worthless lives. The apostle calls them in this our lesson "sons of disobedience," because those thus called love disobedience. But he would also have us understand that the sons of disobedience are the children of wrath, and God's wrath ends in death. God tells us this, that He may save us from it. He would have us understand that disobedience will end in utter extinction of being, and that all those who are like-minded will be found at the last children of wrath.

II. From Death to Life. Verses 4-10.

"But God,[1] being rich in mercy, for His great love wherewith He loved us, even when we were dead through our trespasses, made us alive together with Christ (by grace have ye been saved), and raised us up with Him [2] and made us to sit with Him [3] in the heavenly places, in Christ Jesus: that in the ages to come He might show the exceeding riches of His grace [4] in kindness toward us in Christ Jesus: for by grace [5] have ye been saved through faith; and that not of yourselves,[6] it is the gift of God; not of works, that no man should glory.[7] For we are His workmanship,[8] created in Christ Jesus for good works,[9] which God afore prepared that we should walk in them."

NOTE AND COMMENT

1. **"But God."**—In this lies the hope of humanity. Notwithstanding the awful condition of the children of men and their utter hopelessness so far as man is concerned, in God there is hope. First, He is rich in mercy toward the sons of disobedience; secondly, His great love wherewith He loved us moves Him to do all in His power that He may save us; and that great love has demonstrated itself in the giving of the Lord Jesus to die that the sinner might be saved. He loved us even when we were dead through our trespasses; that is, when we needed to be loved; saved us when we needed to be saved; mercy extended, when the mercy was needed; and all this made us alive together with Christ, not apart from Him where we are left to ourselves, but with Christ, or, as some of the ancient authorities read, in Christ, in Him who lives forever.

2. **"Raised us up with Him."**— The thought carries us back to the baptism of the believer. So the same apostle, in writing to the Romans, says, "We were buried therefore with Him through baptism into death: that like as Christ was raised from the dead through the glory of the Father, so we also might walk in newness of life. For if we have become united with Him in the likeness of His death, we shall be also in the likeness of His resurrection." Rom. 6:4, 5. And the same thought in another epistle: "If then ye were raised together with Christ, seek the things that are above, where Christ is, seated on the right hand of God." Col. 3:1. But we are not only raised up with Him symbolically in the act of baptism, but to a new life. Keep in mind the thought of the first verse, "And you did He make alive, when ye were dead through your trespasses and sins,"— not alive to the world, to do the world's work, not alive to the passions and lusts and temptations of the world; but, living the new life in Christ Jesus here, despite

the world, living above the world, walking as Christ walked, witnesses to the power of God.

3. "Made us to sit with Him."—Another blessed privilege that He has given to Christians: we are not simply to count ourselves as existing in this life alone. Our adorable Head is in heaven, seated at the right hand of God. All authority is given to Him — He is the "Head over all things to the church" — and while He is there, He has promised His church militant in the earth, "Lo, I am *with you* always, even unto the consummation of the age." Matthew 28:20, margin. He lives in His people. So, as one who had partaken of the new life states, "I have been crucified with Christ; and it is no longer I that live, but Christ liveth in me; and that life which I now live in the flesh I live in faith, the faith which is in the Son of God who loved me, and gave Himself up for me." Gal. 2:20. But while our blessed Lord lives this life with His children, His children are to count themselves as living with Him in the heavens. We do not exalt ourselves to that place, but God in His great goodness and mercy counts us as dwelling with Him,— children of His own care, directly under His own guidance, sitting with Him in the heavenly places in Christ Jesus. These are the foretastes, the earnests, the pledge moneys, of the redemption of His people. They are the assurances of the promise which God will fulfill in the inheritance which He has for His children.

4. "Riches of His grace."—We do not know the exceeding riches of God's grace here. In the very nature of the case, we can not know them. We may appreciate them to some extent. We may lay hold upon them, or apprehend them, but we never can comprehend them. The love and wisdom and power of eternity is in His grace, and it will take eternity to comprehend it. Great and rich was His grace that saved us as sinners. Of that we can comprehend something. It keeps us from sin, and of that, too, we may understand a little; and yet how very little we know of the mighty conflicts of spiritual forces which are waged in order to save those whom Satan claims as his lawful captives of sin!

It will take more than this life to reveal the "riches of His grace;" consequently "the ages to come" await God's children,

—not this age, with its sin, alone; not the judgment age of the thousand years; but all the glorious ages which follow, ages in which sin shall have passed away forever. Then will be revealed anew, over and over, the great creative power of God in bringing new worlds into existence, in which His people, saved by grace from this sinful world, shall have part. In all these will God be showing to His children "the exceeding riches of His grace." But as it is infinite in its depth of wisdom and knowledge, it will take eternity to learn it. As has been remarked, the great plan of salvation shall be the science and the song of eternity.

5. "For by grace."—It is always well to remember it. How natural it is for poor humans to boast that I have never done this, and I never would do that, and I have never stooped to this, or that. They forget the pit from which their own feet have been taken, the very mercy, perhaps, that surrounded their childhood days in kind father and mother who have kept them from sinning. It was John Bunyan who said, as he saw a criminal passing him on his way to execution, "But by the grace of God, there goes John Bunyan." Many of us have not fallen to the low and degrading sins which even the world looks upon as debasing and disgraceful, but we have been kept from them simply through the kindness and favor of God in the restraining influences of the teachings of Christianity, and of firm and faithful friends in our youth. Just as truly as the veritable drunkard or libertine is saved by grace, so must every child of Adam be saved. Like Nicodemus, we may pride ourselves on our morality, but the eternal fact remains, "Except one be born from above, he can not see the kingdom of God." John 3:3, margin. It is not our ancestry or our birth or our works which commend us to God, but our great need; and our great need moved His heart of love and pity to reveal to us through grace, Jesus Christ. "For by grace have ye been saved through faith." Faith has simply yielded to the Master, and thereby opened a channel through which the exceeding grace could come into the heart.

6. "That not of yourselves."—This has been taken by some to refer to the faith, but it seems clearly to refer to the grace, and more to the salvation which has come to us through grace.

By grace we have been saved, and that salvation not of ourselves. We could not purchase it, nor could our friends purchase it for us. It is a truth of the ages that none of us can
by any means save his brother, or give to God a ransom for
him. Psalm 49:7. "All have sinned, and fall short of the
glory of God." All have fallen below the perfect standard, and
shut themselves out from a home in His kingdom; and, therefore, the saving is not of ourselves. It is the gift of God. His
free, unmerited favor has been bestowed upon us. He gave
Himself for our sins. By His death are we reconciled, and by
the power of His endless life we are saved.

7. **"Not of works, that no man should glory."**—We can not
earn salvation. Work as we will, it is impossible for us to rise
above the very nature of the motives which dwell in the selfish
heart of the human. Men have been trying this through all
the weary ages of sin in the past. The long pilgrimages that
are made on hands and blistered knees through the hot, sandy
plains of India have been to earn salvation. The lying upon
sharp spikes day after day and week after week, the wearing
of stones in the shoes, the cutting, the lacerating, the long fasts
almost to starvation, the hair shirts, the pitiable ways in which
men have endeavored to mutilate themselves,—all these are
mighty witnesses that there is no salvation in the works of
men. And then, too, it is a denial of the great free grace of
God through our Lord Jesus Christ. If Saint A could say that
he had earned salvation by his works of humiliation and self-
denial and flagellations, he could boast in himself. And if Saint
B could say that he, through his fastings and mortifications of
the flesh, had earned salvation, he could boast in himself; but
in those glorious ages to come there will no one stand up and
say that I have earned salvation. All the pitiful works of men
will be seen to be righteousnesses which are as filthy rags, and
the only garment which will then be acceptable will be the
garment of the righteousness of our Lord Jesus Christ, woven
in the loom of heaven and worked out amid all the temptations
of earth through the perfect, abundant grace and power of God.
And that righteousness of God wrought out in Him will cover
all the sins of the past, and that life of God flowing out through

Him will enable the sinner to live the righteous life; and the glory will be all given to the Master.

8. "For we are His workmanship."—All these expressions are connected with the great gift of His grace,—"for by grace have ye been saved," "for we are His workmanship." They are the reasons for glorying in His grace, reasons for taking no glory to ourselves. For if we are changed beings, born from above, it is His own creative power that has wrought the work. And how clearly this scripture shows that redeeming power is creative power! Salvation by works is the power of evolution demonstrated through all the ages to be utterly futile in the salvation of men and in the formation of character. But salvation by the creative power of God has demonstrated even in the worst characters that the power of God is greater than all the inherited, transmitted, and fostered traits of character of the sinner. It re-creates the drunkard, and it gives him a new life. It takes away the appetite from the flesh, or gives him power to live above it. It makes the covetous man a liberal man, the profane man a reverent man, the niggardly, stingy man a generous man, the dishonest man honorable, the one who has hated his fellow men one who loves them. It removes the old grudges from the heart. In other words, it re-creates all the motives and affections of the soul in Christ Jesus.

How the passage carries us back, as do many other expressions in the New Testament, to the very beginning, to the bringing from chaos to cosmos of this old world, to the Sabbath which God gave to the children of men as a memorial of His creative power, and His use of that very Sabbath as a memorial of sanctifying and redeeming power! Just as He has told us in Ezekiel 20:20: "And hallow My Sabbaths; and they shall be a sign between Me and you, that ye may *know that I am Jehovah your God,*"—your Creator, your Maker, the one to whom you owe all. But more than that, in verse 12, "Moreover also I gave them My Sabbaths, to be a sign between Me and them, that they might know that *I am Jehovah that sanctifieth them.*" The Creator is the only one who can be the Redeemer. The hope of mankind is not in evolution or education; it is in re-creation, in regeneration. But the power that regenerates, the power that re-creates, places the soul on vantage ground in a pabulum of life where there will be growth,— divine evolution and education in Christ Jesus.

9. "For good works."— God has not created us for a life of idleness. There must be no drones in the human hives of God. He has not only the good works for His children, but He has prepared these works before, that we should walk in them,— in that wonderful plan devised of Him before this earth came into existence. At that time must have been written the great book of life, and in that great book of life there must have been the names of the characters that should people the earth, characters that should be "to the praise of the glory of His grace" throughout all eternity: and those characters are to be developed through good works, and the good works that He Himself had marked out, prearranged. The works were marked out and made ready for the development of the character. Consequently, when He called mankind from the great depths of sin and iniquity, He did this that He might create us for the very purpose that we should manifest those good works to the children of men around us on every side. So said Jesus, "Ye are the light of the world. . . . Even so let your light shine before men; that they may see your good works, and glorify your Father who is in heaven." Matt. 5:16. Therefore we read again that Christ "gave Himself for us, that He might redeem us from all iniquity, and purify unto Himself a people for His own possession, *zealous of good works.*" Titus 2:14.

But in those good works His children will not boast, because "it is God who worketh in you both to will and to work, for His good pleasure." Phil. 2:13. In fact, those who are living the nearest the Master, those who are devotedly and earnestly serving Him the best, see more and more of imperfection in the service which they render. They are more inclined to say, "I am an unprofitable servant," rather than to say, "See the mighty works which I have wrought." But the great God who understands the spirit and motive of His children notes the heart that is in the works, and will say to them at last, "Well done, good and faithful servant." They have appropriated His great grace, and He gives them credit as though they wrought it all.

III. It Is Well to Remember. Verses 11, 12.

"Wherefore remember, that once ye, the Gentiles [1] in the flesh, who are called Uncircumcision by that which is called Circumcision, in the flesh, made by hands; that ye were at that time [2] separate from Christ, alienated from the commonwealth of Israel, and strangers from the covenants of the promise, having no hope and without God in the world."

NOTE AND COMMENT

1. **"Gentiles."**— We are sure the student will comprehend the terms used: "Gentiles," all those who are outside of Israel, called also Uncircumcision by the Jews; while the Jews are represented by what is called Circumcision, having the mere outward marking of the people of God. Later on, the Gentiles are spoken of as those that are afar off, and the Jews as those that are nigh. The real contrast between the people of the world, however, and the people of God is not national or outward token, but character and spirit.

2. **"At that time."**— It is hoped that the reader will mark the clear and tremendous distinction which the apostle makes between the unconverted and the converted man. Language could not make stronger the contrast, or the hopelessness of those who have not yielded themselves to God. There is much talk in these days over divine immanence,— men having life in themselves, God dwelling within men, etc., until the world is coming to believe, through the various deceptions that there are, that man has it within his own power to work out his own salvation, and that the power to which he is to look is the god within him, and not the God above him.

The apostle here makes it just as strong as language can convey the idea, that he who stands by himself, who does not believe in the gospel of the Lord Jesus Christ, who is not made alive through the power of God, that in that condition he is (a) separate from Christ; (b) alienated from Israel — the prevailers by faith; (c) strangers from God's covenant of promise; (d) having no hope, and without God in the world. That is the condition of all who are outside of Christ, and by "outside of Christ" we do not mean all those who have not the fullest knowledge of the great plan of salvation, but all those who have not yielded themselves to God, for Him to will and to work and to lead and to guide according to His own great purpose.

IV. In Christ Jesus. Verses 13-18.

"But now [1] in Christ Jesus ye that once were far off are made nigh in the blood of Christ. For He is our peace, [2] who made both one, and brake down the middle wall of partition, having abolished [3] in His flesh the enmity, even the law of commandments contained in ordinances; [4] that He might create in Himself [5] of the two one new man, so making peace; and might reconcile them both in one body unto God through the cross, having slain the enmity thereby: and He came and preached peace [6] to you that were far off, and peace to them that were nigh: for through Him [7] we both have our access in one Spirit unto the Father."

NOTE AND COMMENT

1. **"But now."**—It is a wonderful change that is wrought in the believer. Expressing it elsewhere, the apostle declares, They are delivered out of the power of darkness and translated into the kingdom of the Son of His love. Col. 1:13. It is expressed more lightly here, but nevertheless decidedly, that in Christ Jesus, although once far off, they are now made nigh. He stands for them, and they are seen in Him — reconciled by His death, washed white in the blood of the Lamb.

2. **"He is our Peace."**—"There is no peace, saith Jehovah, to the wicked." Isa. 48:22. His heart is like the troubled sea that "can not rest, and its waters cast up mire and dirt." Isa. 57:20, 21. In the words of the apostle, "Because the carnal [fleshly] mind is enmity against God: for it is not subject to the law of God, neither indeed can be." Rom. 8:7, A. V. Remember always that God is not at enmity with the sinner. "I know the thoughts that I think toward you, saith Jehovah, thoughts of peace, and not of evil, to give you hope in your latter end." Jer. 29:11. And therefore He proclaims, "Peace, peace, to him that is far off and to him that is near, saith Jehovah; and I will heal him." Isa. 57:19. God's word abounds in the messages of peace. God's peace in Christ Jesus

is waiting every troubled heart. "This Man shall be our peace," not only when He shall come again, but even now and forevermore. Micah 5:5.

Therefore all who accept Christ Jesus with all their hearts find peace with God. He broke down the middle wall of partition — sin — that separated man from God and man from man, and makes us by grace through faith one with Him, the only way in which Christians can be made one,— bound together in the bond Christ Jesus, first of all, one in Him, and then one with each other because one in Him, fulfilling His prayer, "That they may all be one; even as Thou, Father, art in Me, and I in Thee, that they also may be in Us." John 17:21.

3. "Having abolished."—The thing which He abolishes is the enmity, and the place where He abolishes it is in His flesh. Jesus Christ took upon Himself the flesh of those whom He saves. "Since then the children are sharers in flesh and blood, He also Himself in like manner partook of the same." Heb. 2:14. "God sent forth His Son, born of a woman, born under the law, that He might redeem them that were under the law." Gal. 4:4, 5. "Who was born of the seed of David according to the flesh." Rom. 1:3. Therefore the flesh which He took was the flesh that possessed all the tendencies toward sin, just the same as the flesh which the children bear; and that flesh, if its tendencies had been followed, would have led our Lord into sin as it has led every human being into sin; but by the power of the Spirit of God dwelling in Him by faith that enmity was overthrown. The only reason in the world why man does not overcome is because of the carnal mind, or the mind of the flesh, for "the mind of the flesh is enmity against God; for it is not subject to the law of God, neither indeed can it be." Rom. 8:7. Man has yielded his mind to the flesh,— nay, more than that, he has willingly done this, until the mind that he has is not the spiritual mind, but the fleshly mind. The mind is in bondage to sin. Our Lord began His work where man failed,— in the mind; and there He abolished the enmity in the flesh.

4. "Contained in ordinances."— Out of the carnal, fleshly, selfish mind have grown the laws of ordinances, which man has made from time immemorial. He hopes to save himself by such ordinances as "handle not, nor taste, nor touch." See Col. 2:20-23. The law of ordinances that the Jews knew, the ceremonial law of the Levitical age, bound about by Pharisaical tradition and loaded with added ceremonies and impositions, had lost its significance as a body of types and shadows of the real in Christ Jesus. These laws were not designed to set Israel at enmity to the Gentile world nor the Gentile world at enmity to Israel. All the precepts given by God were to separate God's people unto Himself, separate from sin, revealing to the nations around in precept, faith, life, and love, the excellence of Jehovah manifest upon and through a faithful and devoted people. The standard of the holy law should be guarded; the gospel in type must be maintained. But all these did not shut out one believing Gentile. See Deut. 4:2-8; 1 Kings 8:41-43, and other scriptures. But the Jews compromised and lost, and made God's good laws into a Pharisaical fence or wall, shutting out the nations and exalting themselves as nationally the elect of God. Some of the laws of the typical service became, in the mind of the Jew, means of salvation rather than mere types and forms of expressions of faith, and, thus used, they separated man from God rather than brought man to Him.

When Jesus came, type met antitype. The age of the Aaronic priesthood terminated at the cross. The promised Messiah came of the tribe of Judah. Still the old wall remained as it had for years. It was true in its divine foreshadowing, but it became a barrier of selfishness, showing forth the enmity of the unregenerate heart of which it became a fit symbol. Jesus by His death abolished, made of none effect, void, or empty, that perverted system.

5. "Create in Himself."— God's object is to unify. He is one, and our blessed Lord is one, and His plan is one. There are no classes in the great saved throng around His throne. The family in earth and heaven is one. It is not God's design that there shall be a great number of churches and congregations and sects and peoples. He has not one method of salvation for the Jew and another for the Gentile. Our Lord Himself steps in and creates in Himself of the two one new

man. He makes peace between the great world factions of
Jew and Gentile, or whatever they may be called, by uniting
them both in Him, and in Him reconciling them both in one
body unto God through the cross, through the crucifixion of
the flesh, through the slaying of the carnal man, through the
putting away of all enmity to God, and yielding to Him in
absolute self-surrender. There is no disunion between the
nationalities according to the flesh that make up God's true
children. The great reason why there is not union at the
present time is that we shun the cross, we do not wish the
enmity to die.

6. **"He came and preached peace."**— That is the message of
the gospel —"Peace on earth, good will toward men." These
are the good tidings of great joy which God has given to all
people, that there is a way by which all men can make peace
with the Ruler of the universe, and whatever may be the petty
conditions surrounding us in this world, we may stand clear
and true and strong eternally with the One who rules over all.
Let us repeat it again, There is not one salvation for the Jew
and another for the Gentile; there is not one moral code for
the Jew and another for the Gentile; there is not one Sabbath
for the Jew and another for the Gentile. The preaching of
peace through surrender to God's law and the abolition of the
enmity of the carnal heart is that which must come to every
soul, putting all on the same basis of sinfulness, presenting to
all the same terms of forgiveness by repentance and faith, and
creating in all the same kind of heart, one that is obedient to
all God's precepts.

7. **"For through Him."**— It all comes through our Lord
Jesus Christ. He it is who bestows upon us the Comforter,
and in that Comforter, in that life, we have access unto the
Father. Heaven itself is open to us, and the God of all grace
pours out to us its exceeding riches. Compare with Romans 5:2.

V. God's Living Temple. Verses 19-22.

"So then [1] ye are no more strangers and sojourners, but ye are fellow
citizens with the saints, and of the household of God, being built [2] upon the
foundation of the apostles and prophets, Christ Jesus Himself being the chief

Corner Stone; in whom each several building, fitly framed together, groweth [a] into a holy temple in the Lord; in whom ye also [4] are builded together for a habitation of God in the Spirit."

NOTE AND COMMENT

1. "So then."—The apostle presents to us the change that is wrought in the believing Gentile and Jew. All class has gone forever, the Gentiles have come in, and the believing Jew has proved himself to be an Israelite in reality, a prevailer by faith. Gen. 32:28; Hosea 12:3, 4. The Gentile is no more a stranger, no more a sojourner, but a fellow citizen with the believing Jew, and between fellow citizens there are no distinctions or discriminations as citizens. He is a fellow citizen with the saints, nay, more,— the apostle brings it home in still closer relationship,— he is not only a fellow citizen so far as the government is concerned, but he is of the household of God, a member of the divine family. Sons and daughters of the Most High are the believers. There could be no clearer, stronger expression of relationship.

2. "Being built."— God does not leave His children unestablished, or to die. They are built upon something which endures, and this foundation is the foundation of the apostles and prophets,— not one which the apostles and prophets laid, but upon which the apostles and prophets have builded, the Rock of the living God. Matt. 16:16-18. The chief corner stone is our Lord Jesus Christ, and the chief corner stone is not a corner stone alone, but it is a foundation stone as well, and therefore we read, "Behold, I lay in Zion for a foundation a stone, a tried stone, a precious corner stone of sure foundation: he that believeth shall not be in haste." Isa. 28:16. The apostle Peter, referring to this very passage in Isaiah, declares that the believers, "as living stones, are built up a spiritual house, to be a holy priesthood, to offer up spiritual sacrifices, acceptable to God through Jesus Christ."

3. "Groweth."— Not only does God establish His children, but they are progressive as well. Stones alone would leave us a wrong idea. They must be living stones. Not only that, but each stone is in itself an individual building,— it is a living building by itself, in whom each several building — that is,

each individual believer — fitly framed together by the Spirit of God, groweth into a holy temple, or sanctuary, in the Lord. Only God's grace is able to do this. Only God's power can shape and mold human characters so that they shall perfectly fit together. Only His life can bind them into one. But thus shaped, molded, and united, they become a holy temple in the Lord. "For in one Spirit were we all baptized into one body, whether Jews or Greeks, whether bond or free; and were all made to drink of one Spirit." 1 Cor. 12:13.

4. "Ye also."— This is the precious thought and the climax of our entire study, that we also, having once walked according to the course of this world, who were once dead in trespasses and sins, who were once separate from Christ, aliens from the commonwealth of Israel, having no hope, and without God in the world,— even we are, through the grace of the Lord Jesus Christ, brought together and builded together for a habitation of God in the Spirit. This is the marvelous grace of Him who worketh all things after the counsel of His own will, who is able to take the most unpromising creatures in His whole universe and make them "to the praise of the glory of His grace" in Christ Jesus. There is a great, comforting contrast between the "ye" of verse one and the "ye also" of verse 22.

IMPORTANCE OF DECISION

Once to every man and nation comes the moment to decide,
In the strife of Truth with falsehood, for the good or evil side;
Some great cause, God's new Messiah, offering each the bloom or blight,
Parts the goats upon the left hand, and the sheep upon the right,
And the choice goes by forever 'twixt that darkness and that light.

—James Russell Lowell.

CHAPTER THREE

Development of the Mystery: Analysis

I. A new revelation. Verses 1-6.
II. More of the mystery. Verses 7-13.
III. Prayer for the fullness of blessing. Verses 14-21.

I. A New Revelation of the Mystery. Verses 1-6.

"For this cause [1] I Paul, the prisoner of Christ Jesus in behalf of you Gentiles,— if so be that ye have heard [2] of the dispensation of that grace of God which was given me to youward; how that by revelation [3] was made known unto me the mystery, as I wrote before in few words, whereby, when ye read, ye can perceive my understanding in the mystery of Christ; [4] which in other generations was not made known [5] unto the sons of men, as it hath now been revealed unto His holy apostles and prophets in the Spirit; to wit, that the Gentiles [6] are fellow heirs, and fellow members of the body, and fellow partakers of the promise in Christ Jesus through the gospel."

NOTE AND COMMENT

1. **"For this cause."**— The apostle refers back to what had been previously said. He had just told these Gentile believers that they were built into the household of God, members of the commonwealth of Israel, no more strangers to the covenants of promise. This is a part of Paul's preface to the wonderful prayer that he has for them. **"The prisoner of Christ Jesus."**— Paul's earnest desire for the Gentiles led to the enmity, jealousy, and hatred of the Jews, and this led to his imprisonment. However, he does not look upon it as something which he should hold against the Jews, but a part of the work of the Lord Jesus Christ who called him. He was told, in the very beginning of his call, of the things that he must suffer for Christ's sake, and those were a part of the things which God had appointed, so that while he was a prisoner, he was a prisoner in connection with his work and in behalf of the Gentiles. How blessed it is so to regard the afflictions and trials which come to us! If we look upon them as God's appointment, we shall find blessing in them. If we look upon them as perplexities and trials which we in nowise deserve, and which

some evil-minded person has brought against us, they will cause endless trouble and worry. Rather, let us take them as from the Master — prisoners in behalf of His blessed cause. The apostle preferred to preach to the Jews. He longed to go back to Jerusalem, as we are told again and again in Acts, but God saw in him a chosen vessel, one that could be used mightly in giving light to the Gentiles; and this the apostle ever keeps before him.

2. **"If so be that ye have heard."**—Just a gentle reminder that he had told them of these things. **"The dispensation of that grace of God."**— That is, the divine arrangement, or the disposition, the way, in which God's grace had been revealed, dispensed, and poured out upon the children of men. Of this he tells us all through the first part of his epistle. Doubtless he had given it to these brethren in Ephesus in great detail while he labored among them. He has also given instruction concerning this in his epistles to the Colossians, Philippians, and elsewhere. God had granted to him a dispensation, or a stewardship. Paul himself was to be among those, preëminently, who should dispense, or spread abroad, the news of the blessings of the grace of God. And this, in a measure, is given to every one according to his ability.

3. **"By revelation."**— The apostle did not receive his gospel through Jesus as He walked here in the flesh, nor did he receive his mission from the other apostles. He informs us in Galatians, the first chapter and the 11th and 12th verses: "For I make known to you, brethren, as touching the gospel which was preached by me, that it is not after man. For neither did I receive it from man, nor was I taught it, but it came to me through revelation of Jesus Christ." The Lord Himself, he tells us, appeared to him as one born out of due time. 1 Cor. 15:8. He, like others, had seen the Lord. An abundance of revelations and visions was given unto him. The whole plan and scheme of God's gospel, as taught in all the prophets of the past and fulfilled in our Lord Jesus Christ, was opened before the apostle.

4. **"The mystery of Christ."**— Not mystery in the sense in which secret society people held mysteries, then and now, but the mystery which God reveals to all those who will come into

fellowship and harmony with Him—"the mystery of the gospel," as stated in the sixth chapter and 19th verse. "The secret of the Lord is with them that fear Him; and His covenant to make them know it." Ps. 25:14, margin.

5. "Not made known."— Not long had this fullness of the gospel been known, yet it had been known sufficiently so that souls could embrace it and live. That has been demonstrated in every generation by the believers in God, and in His plan to save. Righteous Abel was a witness to his generation as against Cain, the unbeliever. Enoch witnessed for God during the time which he lived. Noah witnessed, Abraham witnessed, Melchizedek, Jethro, Moses, and all the believers in Israel, Balaam, the wise men who came from the east,— all the good of all the ages past,— were witnesses to the effectiveness of the plan of salvation, dimly though it was revealed in type and shadow and promise. But the abundance of that revelation did not come until our Lord manifested it in the flesh, showing in His own life the power of God to save and to keep mankind from sin in a world of sin,— that the Seed of the woman could live above all environments; that is the mystery of godliness, God manifest in the flesh. 1 Tim. 3:15.

This mystery had been revealed dimly before, even as the moon reflects the light of the sun, but when the Lord Jesus came, He revealed it in far fuller measure; and the weakened, wicked world needed the greater, the brighter, the clearer, revelation. But this will be revealed — in the last great day it will be seen — that there has been light enough, always, for men to come to the true Light if they would but receive it. Yet there is more of the light of God. They make a fatal mistake who interpret God's promises to Israel of old in the dimmer light of the typical system regardless of the later light through Jesus and His apostles. For, "the path of the righteous is as the dawning light, that shineth more and more unto the perfect day." Even unto the end of this world's probationary period, floods of light will be poured out upon God's people. Blessed is the man who, by fresh supplies of life, keeps the wine skin of heart and mind fresh and expansive to the new wine of God's truth.

6. "The Gentiles."— It is strange, in the light of such scriptures as this, that men will contend that God has one plan for the Jew and another for the Gentile; that He makes a difference between the two; that, if He has the gospel for one, He has more than the gospel for the other; and that for the Jew He has a higher position in the closing days of the Christian dispensation than He has for the Gentile. There are promises and prophecies in the Old Testament concerning the Jews which are difficult to be understood. There are prophecies of the restoration of Israel which would seem to indicate that the Jews are to be restored again to their own land; but, in the light of the clearer later revelation, all these things are plain. All the Old Testament prophecies may be classified under one of three heads: either they were fulfilled in the establishment of the Jews in their own land before or after the Babylonian captivity; or they were typical prophecies, fulfilled in part to the Jews there, but to be fulfilled in the completest sense with the true Israel of God under Christ; or they were conditional prophecies in which the Jews never met the conditions, and which, of course, God could not fulfill to them. See Jer. 18:7-10.

But when our Lord Jesus Christ came, and was rejected of the Jews, there were of necessity new developments foretold in the carrying out of God's purpose. Not but that His purpose has been always the same, but the nation that was to hold together during all the centuries until the Messiah should appear had accomplished its end, and from that time on it must stand in the same relationship to Him as all other nations; and therefore all who come in from all other nations are of the Israel of God, built upon the foundation of the apostles and prophets, both Jew and Gentile by faith,— the Gentile a fellow heir and fellow member of the body, the church,— and a fellow partaker of all the promises in Christ Jesus. "And if ye are Christ's, then are ye Abraham's seed, heirs according to promise." Gal. 3:29. "For they are not all Israel, that are of Israel: neither, because they are Abraham's seed, are they all children: but, In Isaac shall thy seed be called. That is, it is not the children of the flesh that are children of God; but the children of the promise are reckoned for a seed." Rom. 9:6-8.

In the gospel of Jesus Christ, in the fold of God, there is neither Jew nor Greek, barbarian nor Scythian, bond nor free, but Christ is all in all.

II. More of the Mystery. Verses 7-13.

"Whereof I was made a minister, according to the gift of that grace of God which was given me according to the working of His power.[1] Unto me, who am less[2] than the least of all saints, was this grace given, to preach[3] unto the Gentiles the unsearchable riches of Christ; and to make all men see what is the dispensation of the mystery which for ages hath been hid in God[4] who created all things; to the intent that now unto the principalities and the powers in the heavenly places might be made known through the church the manifold wisdom of God,[5] according to the eternal purpose[6] which He purposed in Christ Jesus our Lord: in whom we have boldness and access in confidence through our faith[7] in Him. Wherefore I ask that ye may not faint at my tribulations for you, which are your glory."

NOTE AND COMMENT

1. **"The working of His power."**— It is God's power that the apostle magnifies; and the gift that was bestowed upon him as apostle and as a minister of God's grace was not because of Paul's achievement, but was wholly of God. So every disciple can say; for every child of His has been made a partaker of the grace given through Christ, and behind that grace and in its ministration all the power of God is pledged to His disciple.

2. **"Who am less."**— Note that the apostle's glory does not extend to himself. He is not saying, with the new-thought disciples of the present day, "I am," and "I am power," "I am great," and "I am light," and "I am all that God is." Such words are blasphemous. The apostle Paul declared that he was less than the least of all saints, literally, "more least than all the saints;" and yet to him God gave this great grace, and he magnifies the grace, and he magnifies the power of God. It would be a denial of God to do otherwise; and it would also be a denial of God to magnify himself.

3. **"To preach."**—The margin reads, "to bring good tidings unto the Gentiles;" in other words, to carry the gospel. He gives it another term here, "the unsearchable riches of Christ." That is what the gospel brings. There is absolutely no limit

to its power, to its blessings. No word of inspiration places a limit upon it. It is able to save to the uttermost, and able to satisfy the hungriest soul. By the term "unsearchable" is not meant that which we can not search, but it means that which by all searching we can not fathom or comprehend. We may find the riches, and we may enjoy them. So persons do in this world sometimes concerning the riches that perish; but sometimes those with vastly more than a competence, with wealth enough to enable them to live affluently until they die, yet are worrying because they know the limit of their wealth. The Christian need not have that worry; he may be so poor that he feels that he is less than the least; he may be so unworthy that he feels that he is not entitled to a farthing of God's wealth; but if he accepts the gospel and has faith in the Master, there is no end to the riches to which faith opens the door, either in this world or in the world to come. It was these unsearchable riches of which the apostle is telling the story, and not only that, but to make all men see, or to bring to light to all men, "the dispensation of the mystery."

4. "Which for ages hath been hid in God."—Yet in those ages past men learned of God, and learned of the exceeding riches of His grace. But when Christ, the Son of God, died, they saw more than had ever been comprehended before of the great love of God to men; and when He rose from the dead triumphant, there was revealed not only the love but the power. Even now in a sense they are hid in God; but he who by faith in Christ enters into the divine relationship finds there the hiding of His power. In God is he possessed of all the riches, and to all this the creative power of God is pledged.

Experiments of Grace

5. "The manifold wisdom of God."— The Christian is not working out his problem here for himself alone. The apostle opens a far larger view than this. God's character in the universe is at stake, and there are other worlds watching this little world as it passes through the solution of the great problem of sin; so in the working out of this problem it is God's purpose that the principalities and the powers in the heavenly places might see and know through the church "the manifold wisdom of God," wisdom, variegated, many-sided, many-tinted, meeting all conditions in the glory and beauty of God. God is making experiments in this laboratory of the gospel upon human hearts,— not experiments that are bound one thousand to one to go wrong, as do the experiments of the human scientist before he succeeds, but experiments every one of which is bound to go right if the subject upon which he is working is submissive.

In the experiments of the human the will of the subject is not taken into consideration at all. In the laboratory of the chemist, or in the dissecting room of the vivisectionist, there must be no will to oppose the researches of the scientist; but in God's great laboratory the human will must be taken into account, and even the greatness of God will not step over the circle of freedom which He has drawn around the human. If, however, man will but yield to the eternal purpose, there will be wrought out in him the marvelous working of God triumphant over all sin and over all the effects of sin; for it is His purpose to take of the poor, weakened, wretched, deformed, distorted children of earth, made all they are that is bad by sin, and make them "to the praise of the glory of His grace" through Jesus Christ, and the righteousness of God which He places upon them, and the creative power inwrought in a new being born from above; and that in this work all the heavenly principalities and powers will see the manifold wisdom of God.

Another has wonderfully said: "The Lord Jesus is making experiments on human hearts through the exhibition of His mercy and abundant grace. He is effecting transformations so amazing that Satan, with all his triumphant boasting, with all his confederacy of evil united against God and the laws of His government, stands viewing them as a fortress impregnable to his sophistries and delusions. They are to him an incomprehensible mystery. The angels of God, seraphim and cherubim, the powers commissioned to coöperate with human agencies, look on with astonishment and joy that fallen men, once children of wrath, are through the training of Christ developing characters after the divine similitude, to be sons and daughters of God, to act an important part in the occupations and pleasures of heaven."

All of this, but dimly suggested in the pre-advent days, was clearly manifest in the days of the apostle. The antediluvian age was clearly marked by divine plan and interference. So also was the patriarchal age, and so also the Levitical, by its priesthood, and likewise the Christian age. When the antediluvian age ended, it would seem as though God's plan were utterly thwarted; and yet faith said that out of the things not seen God would make to appear the things which He had promised. When the patriarchal age ended, the descendants of Abraham to whom the promise came were in sore bondage to the mightiest power that earth knew, and were there a nation of slaves; yet faith said that out of the things not seen God would bring the promises to the fathers. When Jehovah triumphed over all the power of Egypt, it was by an aged man, a shepherd for forty years who had forgotten his knowledge of the Egyptian tongue, and a rod. But the man was "the man of God" and the rod was "the rod of God," wholly His, and He wrought salvation out of the unseen.

When the Levitical age ended, the very Prince of life Himself had died upon the cross, and was locked in the stone sepulcher and sealed with a Roman seal; yet faith said, even in the one who died beside Him on the cross, that not out of things appearing should that which is seen have come into existence. From the very death God brought life, and through that death salvation to all His children. Heb. 2:14.

Even so the present age will seem to end in world triumph. Apostasy, which has reared its head in more or less limited success in the past ages, will in the last days sing, "I sit a queen, and am no widow, and shall in nowise see mourning," and shall dare to say, "I am, and there is none else besides me." Rev. 18:7; Isa. 47:8. But the very triumph of apostasy is the prelude to its destruction; and then shall appear the Lord Jesus Christ to bring to naught the things that are, that no flesh should glory in His presence. So it will be at the close of the judgment age of the one thousand years. Satan, with all his hosts of wickedness which are raised from the dead, will think that he is able to take the mighty seat of God, which has descended upon a desolated earth; but the glory of

God will destroy sin and all identified with sin, and the eternal age of the ages which the people of God have seen by faith shall begin its glorious cycles, nevermore to know sin or death.

God's Purpose of the Ages

6. "According to the eternal purpose."—Literally, "according to the purpose of the ages;" and this purpose of the ages, we are told, was purposed in Christ Jesus our Lord. The infinite God foresaw all the things which would arise, the rebellion which would enter His empire, the steps which would and must be necessary in order to convince men, in spite of every misrepresentation of His character, that God is love; and all these various steps were marked off in the history of this world: the antediluvian age and its climax in rebellion; the purpose of the call of Abraham, and the segregation of the families through which the Seed was to come, the patriarchal age; the calling of a people out from Egypt into the Promised Land, there, notwithstanding all their rebellion, to be held through all the years till the Son of God was born of a woman, the Levitical age; followed by what is commonly called the Christian age, in which the gospel should be preached to all the world and to every nation, with no people or center chosen for the manifestation of God's glory, this to terminate with the judgment, and finally the restoration of all things promised by His holy prophets. Thus we have the antediluvian age, the patriarchal age, the Levitical age, the Christian age, the judgment age and its execution covering the millennium, the great "day of Jehovah," and the eternal ages of ages. These were constituted in the beginning, and throughout all this great purpose God has been working out the successive revelations of the mystery. See Eph. 3:11; Heb. 1:2; 11:3, margin.

Seemingly every age has ended in defeat of God's plan. Looking at it from the purely human standpoint, the close of each age predicted hopeless defeat; but faith in God has grasped the unseen things and triumphed. With this thought in mind we can better understand Hebrews 11:3: "By faith we understand that the worlds [literally, "ages"] have been framed by the word of God, so that which is seen hath not been made out of things which appear." Rotherham renders

it: "By faith we understand the ages to have been fitted together by declaration of God, to the end that not out of things
appearing should that which is seen have come into existence."
This is much more a literal translation than our common ver-
sions.   Upon the original word *aion* —"age"— from which
"ages" comes, he has this to say: "The first thing to note is
that the idea of an age is one of comparatively slow growth.
The Biblical parent of the Greek *aion* is the Hebrew *olam,* and
the root conception of *olam* is concealed duration. . . . The
second thing to observe is that duration does not fall into ages
until it acquires character, and there is a transition of the
times from one character into another. . . . The fourth point
of importance is that only as a change of age is supernaturally
superinduced can we assume to characterize and begin age as
a divine dispensation."

7. "Boldness and access . . . through our faith."— We do
not wonder that, as the apostle surveyed the great eternal
purpose of God, he could have boldness in believing in our
Lord Jesus Christ. Surrounding circumstances might be all
against him. The weakness of the flesh itself might be para-
mount. Before him waited the Roman dungeon and the heads-
man's block. He had himself seen in vision the long, desolating
power of the great apostasy; but beyond all this he saw the
glorious triumph of the coming of our Lord Jesus Christ.
Truly he had boldness, truly he had access to God and confidence through faith in Him! and, in the light of all this, he
could earnestly ask that others, looking upon him and upon
his persecutions, might not faint at his tribulations, which
were for their glory after all, because through those very
things Paul had brought the gospel to them, the gospel which
would result, if they held fast, in their eternal salvation.

III. Prayer for the Fullness of Blessing. Verses 14-21.

"For this cause [1] I bow my knees unto the Father, from whom every
family [2] in heaven and on earth is named, that He would grant [3] you, according to the riches of His glory, that ye may be strengthened with power
through His Spirit in the inward man; that Christ may dwell [4] in your hearts
through faith; to the end [5] that ye, being rooted and grounded in love, may
be strong to apprehend with all the saints what is the breadth and length and

height and depth, and to know the love of Christ which passeth knowledge, that ye may be filled [6] unto all the fullness of God.

"Now unto Him that is able [7] to do exceeding abundantly above all that we ask or think, according to the power that worketh in us, unto Him [8] be the glory in the church and in Christ Jesus unto all generations forever and ever. Amen."

NOTE AND COMMENT

1. "For this cause."— Not tribulations referred to in the verse previous, but the great plan of God, the revelation of the unsearchable riches of Christ, the bringing of all men to the great, eternal purpose of God. "For this cause" embraces all this wonderful revelation which the apostle has been giving, and because of this it is that he bows to the great Father of all in pleading for his disciples. Our Common Version has "the Father of our Lord Jesus Christ," and so has the Syriac; but the best Greek copies omit this. Whether it belongs to the text or not does not make any change in the theology. God is called elsewhere "the Father of our Lord Jesus Christ," emphasizing the brotherhood of man with Him. But it is to the Father, in either way, that the apostle bowed his knees, and that we would do well to bow ours, and plead that the same prayer which he prays may be fulfilled in our behalf.

2. "Every family."—The margin reads "every fatherhood." God's great universe is one. There are not various universes and various gods; but there is one God, the Father of all, the One from whom all things come, the One who rules over all; and every other community of sentient, rational, responsible creatures in all His universe, angels or men, had their origin and being in Him. Just now there is a break in His plan, seemingly, because of sin. Families in heaven and earth seem not to be united. Earth is separated from the great continent of heaven by its gulf of rebellion. Nevertheless this has all been bridged by Jesus Christ, and sometime it will be fully restored. And then the fatherhood of God as regards the entire universe will be seen in the fullness and clearness of which men can only dream now.

3. "That He would grant,"— not according to our poor conceptions, or the little faith that we may have. The apostle's prayer reaches out beyond all this, and prays that God may

grant according to "the riches of His glory," grant according
to an inexhaustible fountain from which to draw. Giving does
not impoverish God. The mighty creative power which is in
Himself is an all-supply at all times for all that He bestows;
and God would have our faith grasp that thought,— that He
gives according to His riches in glory, and out of these riches
of glory, to strengthen God's children with His power through
the mighty Spirit in the inward man. We may not look elsewhere for the fulfillment of this prayer. We may not expect
that it will be carried out through worldly organizations, or
political schemes, or plans of men. It comes by His Spirit,
"the Spirit of Him that raised up Jesus from the dead." Rom.
8:11. See also Eph. 1:20, 21. It is infinite power for which
the inspired prayer petitions.

4. "That Christ may dwell."— Christ the Word, and the
living Word of God dwelling in the heart is Christ in us. See
Psalm 119:11; John 6:63. The Spirit is the Spirit of Christ,
and the indwelling of the Spirit in the inward man is the
indwelling of the Christ; but it is faith which opens the door,
it is faith which bids the Saviour come in, it is faith which
holds Him there. The Syriac connects the last clause of verse
16 with verse 17. After praying that God's children might "be
strengthened with might by His Spirit," this follows the
semicolon: "That in your inner man the Messiah may dwell
by faith, and in your hearts by love, while your root and your
foundation waxeth strong." The thoughts are in a way par-
allel,— the Spirit in the inner man, and Christ dwelling in the
heart. The heart is the seat of the affections. Christ dwelling
in the heart gives us the love of Christ. The Spirit is the life
and the power; and that, dwelling in the inner man, gives us
power over sin. See 2 Cor. 4:16; 1 Peter 3:4.

5. "To the end."—There is a purpose in Christ's dwelling in
our hearts. It is not simply for the joy and comfort of God's
children. It is not simply to make it easy or pleasant. But it
is that the child of God may be rooted and grounded in love,
may sink the great pillars of his faith down to the solid rock,
may strike roots through all surface desert, and take hold upon
the very springs of unseen life and love, that he may from the

lowest pit of disaster and defeat see the triumphant, patient Christ pleading His love and sacrifice for him, that his heart may be stablished in God, and thus rooted and established, may be strong to apprehend with all the saints what is the breadth and length and height and depth of His goodness and power.

The Syriac has, instead of "apprehend," "explore." It is a beautiful thought. Exploring expeditions are always of inter- est to the live, healthy soul; and God wants His children to be ever exploring the breadth and length and height and depth of His great knowledge and wisdom and power and love. They will never reach the end. They will never find limitation in any direction.

Not comprehend, but apprehend. To comprehend is to un- derstand on all sides, to be able to examine all around. We comprehend human things, because we can encompass them, but not so the infinite love and power of God; but we may apprehend, lay hold upon them. We may make them ours; we may seize them in the strong grasp of simple faith, and hold them with us. And this embraces the love of Christ which passes knowledge.

The prayer is an inspired prayer. It is designed for fulfill- ment. It prays that we may search the unsearchable, that we may know the unknowable, that which passes knowledge;— not that we may know of it, not that we may know all there is in it, but that we may truly know it. Jesus says, "My sheep hear My voice." They know His voice. They do not know all its possibilities, all its depths, all its beauty; but they do know it so as to know its character and what it means. Chris- tian men know the love of Christ, know it so that they need never be swerved from it. Never will they comprehend it until eternity is past.

6. **"May be filled."**—This is the climax, the summing up of the prayer,— that God's children "may be filled unto all the fullness of God." That does not mean that the human soul can include all the wisdom and the knowledge and the power of God; but it does mean that all that there is of him will be filled to its fullness with the divine. As much as he is capable of receiving, God designs that he shall receive; and not only

that, but the reception of these divine things will enlarge heart and mind, and enable him to grasp more and more. The power over sin will be complete. The fullness of God will enable him to meet all the temptations of the enemy, and rise victor over all the power of sin. Such is the inspired prayer which God has given for His children.

7. "Him that is able."—All He has promised directly or impliedly, He is able to perform,—nay, beyond our poor asking, because we can only ask for what we see, and we can not see the infinite things which God has for us. We can ask only what we would think; but the human thought is exceedingly limited. It can not think the great infinite things of God, only in the most limited way, while God is able to do exceeding abundantly, superabundantly (The word is a compound of beyond, over and above.—Vincent.), above all that we ask or think; and all this which God is able to do for us He will do according to the power that works in us, which is the power that raised our Lord Jesus Christ from the dead.

8. "Unto Him."—Unto the One who has loved with infinite love, who has sacrificed even life itself, who has given us all things that we enjoy,—"unto Him be the glory in the church"—not only in the church militant, but in the church triumphant—"and in Christ Jesus unto all generations forever and ever;" or, as the margin reads, "all the generations of the age of the ages." Surely to all this we can respond, with the apostle, "Amen."

CHAPTER FOUR

The Divine and the Human: Analysis

I. A plea for unity. Verses 1-6.
II. Gifts of the Spirit. Verses 7-16.
III. The transfer of life. Verses 17-24.
IV. Reformation of life. Verses 25-32.

I. An Earnest Pleading for Unity. Verses 1-6.

"I therefore,[1] the prisoner in the Lord, beseech you to walk worthily of the calling [2] wherewith ye were called, with all lowliness [3] and meekness, with long-suffering, forbearing one another in love; giving diligence [4] to keep the unity of the Spirit in the bond of peace. There is one body,[5] and one Spirit, even as also ye were called in one hope of your calling; one Lord, one faith, one baptism,[6] one God [7] and Father of all, who is over all, and through all, and in all."

NOTE AND COMMENT

God's Called-Out Ones

1. **"I therefore."**—The apostle Paul has the right to plead. He is the apostle to the Gentiles, and he has sealed his apostleship with suffering for Christ and for the sake of the souls for whom he labored. He therefore refers to himself again as "the prisoner in the Lord." He would let them understand that even the sufferings that he is undergoing, he takes as blessings from God. Having been partaker in Christ's sufferings for them, he can truly plead with them that they should honor Christ, and walk worthily of *the calling* wherewith they were called. And then think of that calling.

2. **"Calling."**—The Greek name of the church, *ekklesia,* is from the verb *ekkaleo,* meaning "to call out," or "to summon forth;" and the church itself is an assembly of the citizens regularly summoned by the One who has authority to summon. So God's people are called out of sin and darkness and woe and misery and death; called out from idolatry; called out from everything that is low and base and evil; called by the voice of God, the gospel of God, the Spirit of God, and called out always and forever to better things. We are "called

to be saints" (Rom. 1:7); "called into the fellowship of His Son Jesus Christ our Lord" (1 Cor. 1:9); called "in peace" (1 Cor. 7:15), from the strife and unrest of sin. From the bondage of sin He has called us to liberty (Gal. 5:13); from the world's uncleanness He has called us to holiness (1 Thess. 4:7); He has called us "out of darkness into His marvelous light" (1 Peter 2:9); we are called from the infamy of sin "unto His eternal glory" (1 Peter 5:10); we are called to His kingdom and glory (1 Thess. 2:12). And so we might multiply passages regarding the calling of the children of God. We are called sons and daughters, heirs of God, fellow citizens with the saints. Truly it may be said, in the language of the apostle, that He has "called us with a holy calling." 2 Tim. 1:9. Surely there is force in the apostle's exhortation to "walk worthily of the calling wherewith ye were called."

3. **"With all lowliness,"**—humility. The whole tendency of the world is in the opposite direction. Men are proud and haughty and arrogant. The true child of God is meek. Jesus was meek. Moses was meek. This does not mean that he was soft and pliable, and yielding to everything that came before him. It does mean, however, that he was teachable under God. "The meek will He guide in justice: and the meek will He teach His way." Ps. 25:9. Meekness is mildness and gentleness of temper, submissiveness not to evil, but to God, a disposition not easily provoked.

The truly meek man is the truly strong man. Many times, he who seems to be strong, and blusters, and resents what are thought to be injuries, is, after all, the weak man. He has not conquered himself, he can not control himself. The meek man may be submissive under injuries, patient under trials, heedless of rebukes or abuse; still, where he believes anything to be right, he will stand like the everlasting rock. He is in service to One who will enable him to stand; namely, God. So the man who walks in lowliness and meekness will be long-suffering and forbearing and patient toward others; and as God has done all this for him, not because of necessity, but because of His love for souls, so will the Christian render obedience to God in love. Let us learn that while we hate the sin, we must not hate the sinner.

4. **"Giving diligence."**—The thought of the Christian life is not one of ease; it is one of activity. Diligence implies earnestness in application. It implies industry, steadfastness, watchfulness. The good things of God are certainly worth the keeping; and the keeping is certainly worth the effort. We are to give "diligence to keep the unity of the Spirit,"—the one Spirit, and the one Spirit binds together into one life all God's children. But it is easy for the human, with his limited knowledge and powers, his inability to see the thoughts and motives of others, to allow to come in that which will break the unity and the harmony that ought to exist in the church of God. Let him give diligence to keep all the irritating things out of his intercourse with others. Let all his efforts be to bind together and strengthen the bond of peace which ought always to exist between the believer and his Lord, so that Christ Himself becomes the bond between the individuals; "for He is our peace, who made both one."

5. **"There is one body."**— That one body is the church; the one Spirit is the life of the church; "for in one Spirit were all we baptized into one body, whether Jews or Greeks, whether bond or free; and were all made to drink of one Spirit." 1 Cor. 12:13. Cherish the blessed thought that we are one body — the body of Christ; and cherish the thought that the life power in that body "shall give life also to your mortal bodies through His Spirit that dwelleth in you." Rom. 8:11; 2 Cor. 4:10, 11. There is **one hope** to which we are called,— the hope which centers in our Lord Jesus Christ. We have learned the prayer in the beginning of these studies, "That ye may know what is the hope of His calling." Eph. 1:18. That hope culminates in our Lord Jesus Christ at His coming; for the same apostle tells us that "we should live soberly and righteously and godly in this present world; looking for the blessed hope and appearing of the glory of the great God and our Saviour Jesus Christ." Titus 2:12, 13. That hope, he tells us in the first chapter and the second verse of Titus, includes the hope of eternal life. It includes becoming like our Lord Jesus Christ physically as well as spiritually. It includes the resurrection from the dead. It includes the eternal inheritance of all God's children. That is the one hope to which we are called.

6. "One Lord."— Not many lords. In the great heathen world there are gods many and lords many. They had no conception of one God who was infinite enough to encompass all things. They divided up all the beneficences and malignancies of nature into different gods, every one demanding different kinds of sacrifices, and some of them the most cruel, even of human sacrifices. But the Christian has one Lord — one Master; not an earthly one, but a heavenly one, who combines in Himself the human and the divine,— one Lord Jesus Christ. **"One faith."**— That is, the faith of Jesus Christ, the faith by which He walked while here, the faith which centers in Him, the faith that lays hold on all the eternal springs of God's word.

"One baptism."— On this Vincent, in his "Word Studies," says: "The external sign of faith, but of no significance without the Lord and the faith. Baptism is emphasized instead of the Eucharist, because the latter assumes and recognizes unity as an established fact; while faith and baptism precede that fact, and are essential to it. Baptism, moreover, is not administered to the church as a body, but to individuals, and therefore emphasizes the exhortation to each member to be in vital union with the whole body." Baptism is the outward marriage ceremony which unites the believer to Christ. Rom. 7:4; Gal. 3:27.

7. "One God."— Over all this great unity of apparent diversity is one God and Father of all. God's great universe is one. There are different suns and systems of suns and clusters of suns in the sidereal heavens, but they are all under the control of the one great Power. Sin has interfered with the unity of God's plan in some measure, and God has suffered it. Therefore we see all creation groaning and travailing in pain together until now. Rom. 8:22. It is manifest in burning sun, in dead wanderers in the heavens, in broken planets, in dead moons, and in a thousand different ways upon this sin-cursed earth. All this is the result of sin, which God has suffered that the inhabitants of the universe may see the evil outworking of sin always. But it shall not always be. The longing of the universe will be met, and the creation that travails in pain itself also "shall be delivered from the bondage of corrup-

tion into the liberty of the glory of the children of God."
Rom. 8:21.

It is for this that God waits. He is over all now; He is
working through all now; He is in all now, in the sense that
He is controlling it to His own glory; and he who waits God's
time will sometime see the fruition of all the operations of
God during the waiting, travailing time. It is His plan, it is
the original plan, that the whole universe shall be holy, that
it shall move on in the everlasting cycles of life in glory. All
who will take themselves out of this plan shall perish, but
those who abide steadfast will be crowned with the glory of
the triumph of the purpose of the ages, and shall see the fin-
ishing of the mystery, all things one through Jesus Christ
our Lord.

II. Gifts for Service. Verses 7-16.

"But unto each one [1] of us was the grace given according to the measure
of the gift of Christ. Wherefore He saith,[2] When He ascended on high, He
led captivity captive, and gave gifts unto men. (Now this, He ascended,
what is it but that He also descended into the lower parts of the earth? He
that descended [3] is the same also that ascended far above all the heavens,
that He might fill all things.) And He gave some to be apostles; [4] and some,
prophets; and some, evangelists; and some, pastors and teachers; for the
perfecting of the saints,[5] unto the work of ministering, unto the building up
of the body of Christ: till [6] we all attain unto the unity of the faith, and of
the knowledge of the Son of God, unto a full-grown man, unto the measure
of the stature of the fullness of Christ: that we may be no longer children,[7]
tossed to and fro and carried about with every wind of doctrine, by the
sleight of men, in craftiness, after the wiles of error; but speaking truth in
love, may grow up [8] in all things into Him, who is the head, even Christ; from
whom [9] all the body fitly framed and knit together through that which every
joint supplieth, according to the working in due measure of each several
part, maketh the increase of the body unto the building up of itself in love."

NOTE AND COMMENT

1. **"Unto each one."**— There are no useless members in the
body of Christ. There are no drones in His hives. Every soul
who receives Christ, receives from Him not alone the Holy
Spirit in general, but at least one spiritual gift in particular.
The apostle Paul does not use the distributive term "every
one," but he brings it home emphatically,—"unto each one,"—

and "unto each one of us was the grace given." Note also that the gift is not bestowed according to men's measure or men's estimate. Some would mark out for themselves great places which God in His wisdom clearly sees they could not fill. Others could use great gifts, but in their timidity and humility think that they can do almost nothing. Infinite Wisdom, who bestows the gift, also takes account of the measure. It is given according to the measure of the gift of Christ, meted out in divine wisdom. We may therefore be sure that if we are Christ's we have some divine gift for service. We may have confidence in Him in the use of that gift; and if the life be truly consecrated, that gift, used for Him, will glorify His name.

2. **"Wherefore He saith."**—That is, God saith. The apostle quotes from Psalm 68:18, a prophecy of Christ, of what God has done for His people, of what He will do. The quotation is direct from the Septuagint Version,—"Thou hast led captivity captive." The margin of our Common Version is, "Thou hast led a multitude of captives." When our Lord gave Himself, He gave Himself for all God's creation. Consequently, He went down to the very lowest depths to which sin can bring a soul; that is, to death. He died and was buried, the portals of the grave closed over Him. Entirely apart from the power of righteousness and life He would have remained there forever. He was victorious, however, in life, over sin, and was therefore victorious over death; for death is but finished sin.

We read in the account of the crucifixion in Matthew that when Jesus died there was a great earthquake, the rocks were rent, and the graves were opened, and at the time of His resurrection many came out from the graves and went into the city and appeared unto many. Matt. 27:51-53. He had broken the power of the grave, and these first fruits demonstrated that He had conquered. The captives of Satan that had been chained by death, because of sin in man, were redeemed and released by the almighty power of the Son of God. He led the captives of Satan captive, and when He ascended, there was sung that prophetic twenty-fourth psalm, "Lift up your heads, O ye gates; and be ye lifted up, ye everlasting doors: and the King of glory shall come in." Thus sang the angel escort of our

Lord and His redeemed captives. The response comes from within the gates, "Who is the King of glory?" and the answer is returned, "Jehovah strong and mighty, Jehovah mighty in battle. Lift up your heads, O ye gates; yea, lift them up, ye everlasting doors: and the King of glory will come in." Once again the question is repeated, "Who is this King of glory?" and the answer is returned, "Jehovah of hosts, He is the King of glory." He has come home for the celebration of His triumph; and the captives that He brings with Him are not the captives of death, but the captives of life released from the chains of death.

3. **"Descended"—"ascended."**—Verses 9 and 10 are one of the apostle's great parentheses. There must be told how Jesus won this victory. Our Lord descended into the very depths, "deeper than the earth," some render, that He might rescue all who would put their trust in Him, and demonstrate the surety of the faith of those who had put their trust in Him during past ages. Ascending, He fills all things. By the fullness of His power and His life and His righteousness He meets every need of the great, needy universe. And all those who are in harmony with His plan — with the infinitely wise, divine plan for the universe — will receive of His fullness to eternal perfection.

4. **"And He gave some to be apostles."**— The "He" is emphatic. It is not the design of this letter to tell us all the gifts bestowed in the church. These are simply named as important and representative. Elsewhere the apostle has given us more of these, as in the 12th chapter of 1 Corinthians and in the 12th chapter of Romans. There are not only apostles and prophets and evangelists and teachers and pastors, but there are miracles and healings and helps and governments, and ministrations of various kinds, tongues, and the interpretation of tongues. Every gift that His people need, and have needed in the past or will need in the future, was bestowed by Christ when He ascended up on high.

As the first of all these gifts, He places that of apostleship. "Apostle" means "one sent," and, of course, the outsending of God's gospel message is the first thing always. Very frequently — almost invariably, it may be said — the one who was called to be an apostle possessed other gifts, sometimes the prophetic gift, the evangelical gift, the teaching gift.

The prophet is one who speaks for God. He bears an authoritative message. An evangelist is one who proclaims the gospel; the pastor, one who cares for the flock; and the teachers, those who instruct in divine things. Sometimes these are blended in one, sometimes they are individualized. Sometimes the very prophet may not be the best teacher, may not have the wisdom of an apostle. A right conception of the gifts which God has bestowed upon His church would help wonderfully in the consideration that would be given the individuals who possess the gifts. Read 1 Corinthians 12, where these gifts are likened to members of the body, where we are told that the members that seem the feeblest are necessary, where everything should be regarded because of the office work which belongs to it, because of the Giver who has bestowed upon it His own divine power and efficiency.

Note these particulars: (1) These gifts do not represent natural, inherited ability. They are given by the Father, Son, and Holy Spirit. Rom. 12:3; 1 Cor. 12:4-6; Eph. 4:8. They are given to each one, to every one, to use *"according to his several ability."* Matt. 25:14, 15. (2) They were given, *"set"* in the church, till Christ should come again. Eph. 4:8, 13; 1 Cor. 12:28; 13:9; Matt. 25:14, 19; Luke 19:12, 13. (3) They are given not according to the choice of the one who receives, but as the Giver will. 1 Cor. 12:11. (4) They are given not for the personal profit of the receiver, but to profit for God. 1 Cor. 12:7; Eph. 4:12. See the parables of the talents and the pounds. (5) The three leading gifts are apostles, prophets, teachers. 1 Cor. 12:28. (6) The exceeding preciousness of these gifts is shown in the parables of the pounds and the talents: in the illustration, the highest denomination of money is taken in each; the Roman pound, the *mina,* worth about $19.25; the Hebrew talent, worth about $30,000. These bestowals are royal gifts of God, even the least.

5. **"For the perfecting of the saints."**— The gifts were needed in apostolic days. They are needed not less now. Proud man does not like to acknowledge his need. He wants to be all-sufficient in himself; yet he could easily understand,

by the simple illustration of his own body, that the various members are needed. The various organs and members of the body do not work for themselves, but for the other members. Each is served by all the others; and so God designed that it should be in His church — each member should be served by all others, and then all are well served.

The perfecting of God's church, the building up of His saints, must come through a recognition of these gifts not in ourselves alone, but in others as well. And there must be that willingness to learn and to receive from others those things in which we ourselves may be lacking; and at the same time, willingness to give to others that which, in His own way, God has bestowed upon us, to make us blessings to others. And so the gifts are "for the perfecting of the saints." They are given "unto the work of ministering," that in all the various and multiplied gifts the fullness of Christ may be manifested in ministry to the world. They are given for the building up of the body of Christ by a continual gathering out from the world into the fellowship of Christ those who will glorify His name, and in developing those who are already in Christ into greater, more efficient, more unselfish laborers.

6. "Till."— How often are we told that these gifts were all right for the apostolic times, and then they ceased! But the apostle does not confine them to that period. In the 25th chapter of Matthew we find the parable of the talents. These talents, the highest denomination of Hebrew money, represent the gifts of God's Spirit. The one who distributed the talents and went away represents the Master, and the talents were to be used until His return; and so the gifts in the church are to be used in the church till Christ shall come the second time,— used there as long as they are needed; and that need continues till the whole church attains to the unity of the faith, or comes in the unity of the faith to "the knowledge of the Son of God, unto a full-grown man, unto the measure of the stature of the fullness of Christ"— Christ the infinitely wise Head, and a responsive body fulfilling all the desires of the mind. The church has not reached her full stature as yet. She does not stand blameless before God. She is not yet without spot, or wrinkle, or any such thing, before His throne. The

gifts of God are needed to make visible the imperfections, cut them away, carve and polish and refine the various members, till they will all reflect and declare to the world the glory of Christ's character.

7. "No longer children."— We love children — that is, normal men and women do. They love the little innocent babe, and the wee, prattling child, and the growing and developing lad and lassie; but they do not want to see them always remain children. It is a most pitiful thing to see a child remain a child. We look for growth; and when we see growth neither in mind nor in body, we know that the person before us is subnormal; there is a lack of development, and our love changes to pity, and hope to utter discouragement. Spiritually, there are those in God's church who never grow. They were little children in Him yesterday; they are the same to-day. Instead of bearing burdens, they are anxious to be borne themselves. Instead of helping others, they are anxious to be helped. Instead of finding real, strong, virile encouragement and enjoyment in doing hard — perhaps onerous — work for God, they wish to be amused, petted, till the professed church is full of little children, old in years but undeveloped spiritually in mind and soul. It is pitiful, isn't it?

But if God's gifts were recognized — if each one of these children, when he comes into the faith, was made to understand that God has bestowed upon him a gift to be used, a talent not to be hidden or buried, how many more would develop into strong, stalwart workers for God! That is the design of all the gifts which God has bestowed,— that the members of His church should be no longer children. They should not be saying, as the children in the market places did, "We piped unto you, and ye did not dance,"— we have played one thing, and you would not play with us. He would not have them carried about with every wind of doctrine, or be like children, amused or influenced by the sleight of men, after the wiles of error. It is not in such a way that God would have His church built; and yet every true, loyal, observing soul knows that it is of these largely that His visible church consists.

8. "But . . . may grow up."— It is the growing church which God desires, "speaking truth in love," or, as the margin reads, "dealing truly in love." "This is the love of God, that we keep His commandments," and speaking in love must eventuate in doing in love; and doing in love is that which develops moral muscle and strong characters. Thus God would have His church "grow up in all things into Him, who is the head, even Christ." He is the beginning and the end, the establisher of the eternal verities of God in the hearts of devoted followers; and if each soul grows up in Him, he will not grow away from his brethren, or the other members of the body. He will find that the Christ to whom he is consciously united is that which binds him the more closely to every other member.

9. "From whom."— The "whom" is Christ. The nourishment must come from Him, the body must drink in of His life. The plan is from Him. The fit-framing and the life-knitting must come from our divine Head, and that divine Head will be assisted by all those various gifts represented by the various joints of the body. Union and organization of various gifts make up the centers in God's work, just as there are nerve centers and blood centers in the body in order to supply its need. The working of the gifts which Christ has given in due measure, the recognition of these gifts from our Lord, supernatural in their giving, requiring supernatural grace in their exercise, will indeed make for the increase of the body and the building up of that body in love.

III. The Transfer of Life. Verses 17-24.

"This I say therefore, and testify in the Lord, that ye no longer walk [1] as the Gentiles also walk, in the vanity of their mind, being darkened in their understanding, alienated [2] from the life of God, because of the ignorance that is in them, because of the hardening of their heart; who being past feeling [3] gave themselves up to lasciviousness, to work all uncleanness with greediness. But ye did not so learn Christ; [4] if so be that ye heard Him, [5] and were taught in Him, even as truth is in Jesus: that ye put away, [6] as concerning your former manner of life, the old man, that waxeth corrupt after the lusts of deceit; and that ye be renewed in the spirit of your mind, and put on [7] the new man, that after God hath been created in righteousness and holiness of truth."

4

NOTE AND COMMENT

1. "No longer walk."— It can not be emphasized too strongly, nor said too frequently, emphasized by constant repetition, that the old life must not be continued. New purposes, new life, a new Master, demand new conduct. Conversion in Christ Jesus means a new man. These who were gathered out from the Gentiles must leave all the vanity and emptiness of the mind with the past, and no longer travel the old road. The evil habits of the flesh must be broken, the members educated, trained to the service of the new Master.

2. "Darkened . . . alienated."— Two reasons are given for the darkness and the alienation. Let us go to the basic one, the hardening of their heart. The hardening of the heart, we learn in Hebrews 3:12, comes by departing from the living God, turning away from His instruction, losing grip upon the great verities of His gospel. The man that turns from duty benumbs his conscience, and hardens his heart; and, because of that hardening of the heart, he increases the ignorance within him. He knows less and less of God. He is turning from the light of truth to the darkness of error, and so turning, and suffering the sin and the darkness and the alienation to come in between himself and God, he alienates himself from the life of God. He has only the animal life of the flesh, and that of a perverted flesh; and the perverted flesh leads on to the other sins of the heathen world. The life of God, actual life, comes through righteous yielding. See 1 John 5:13; 2 Cor. 4:10, 11.

3. "Past feeling."— That is, the conscience is past feeling. When it continues to yield to sin, it yields until at last it can no longer be impressed by truth or holiness. The apostle here is leading us on to the ultimate, showing us just what sin will do to those who yield themselves to it. He gives us an awful picture of the heathen world, of some of the nations which God thought necessary to sweep away, who gave themselves up to all lasciviousness, greedily to work all uncleanness. There was no hope for them, no response in their heart to the holiness and salvation which is in Christ Jesus. It is a fearful thing to be "past feeling."

4. "Ye did not so learn Christ."— Let the thought come to the tempted child of God again and again. "Ye did not so learn Christ." He did not teach us vanity; He did not lead us into darkness; He does not alienate us from the life of God. He does not lead to ignorance of mind or hardening of heart. Keep forever with us the thought of the life which Christ would teach us. Seek Him. Seek Him earnestly, feed on His word, seek the salvation of others.

5. "If so be that ye heard Him."— Gently He instructs them! Of course they heard Him. He calls it to mind in the most tender way. They had heard Paul, they had read the wonderful things that he had sent to them. They had heard him, and were taught in him, the truth as it is in Jesus.

6. "Put away."—All these things of the Gentiles, of the fleshly heart, must be put away,— the "former manner of life." The old man of sin, that which binds and chains and corrupts and destroys, must all be put away. If not, more and more the soul will grow corrupt after the lusts of deceit, for every lust of sin is in its very nature deceptive. It blinds and hardens and stupefies the soul the more it is indulged, and leads more and more to corruption and death.

7. "Be renewed . . . put on."— God does not ask us to go naked; He does not leave us without comfort. He takes away nothing but what He would put something infinitely superior in its place. Therefore in the place of the vanity and darkness and ignorance of mind He renews the spirit of the mind; He puts within it a divine life and power; He makes of the old corrupt man a new man, and places within him the heart new-created in God,— not in lasciviousness or uncleanness, but in righteousness and holiness of truth. Who would not change the one for the other?

IV. Reformation in Life. Verses 25-32.

"Wherefore, putting away[1] falsehood, speak ye truth each one with his neighbor: for we are members one of another. Be ye angry,[2] and sin not: let not the sun go down upon your wrath: neither give place to the devil."[3]

"Let him that stole steal no more:[4] but rather let him labor, working with his hands the thing that is good, that he may have whereof to give to him that hath need. Let no corrupt speech[5] proceed out of your mouth, but such as is good for edifying as the need may be, that it may give grace to them that hear. And grieve not the Holy Spirit [6] of God, in whom we were sealed unto the day of redemption. Let all bitterness, and wrath, and anger, and clamor, and railing, be put away [7] from you, with all malice; and be ye kind [8] one to another, tender-hearted, forgiving each other, even as God also in Christ forgave you."

NOTE AND COMMENT

1. **"Putting away."**— Surely the apostle's exhortation is pertinent, when God has accepted the sinner,— nay, has purchased him with the precious blood of Jesus,— there should be a putting away of everything that is contrary to Him. And right at the very base of this putting away lies falsehood. Put the falsehood away. "Speak ye truth each one with his neighbor." The heart that loves truth, that lives truth, that speaks truth, will invariably find and live with the God of truth. It is easier to reform a thief or a drunkard or a gambler than it is an inveterate liar. Sometimes, of course, the element of falsehood lies at the base of all these other sins. There are those who tell falsehood and persist in it, thinking that it does no harm, until they scarcely know when they are telling lies. They do not know what truth is. If there is one thing that a person who longs to form character for eternity ought to cherish, that thing is truth. It is not always pleasant to tell the truth; sometimes it means humility of heart to us, sometimes it means unpleasant duty toward others. It always ought to be preceded by earnest prayer that truth may be told in a way to bring results for God, and not to stir up the wicked passions of the heart.

There are those who feel that they ought to tell unpleasant truth to others sometimes as a duty, but they put it off and put it off, until they get desperate over it, and then make the matter a great deal worse by the way in which they tell it. There is a way in which, after coming out of the audience chamber of God, with the heart melted and tender, the truth can be told so as to win. Cherish this way of doing, first of all putting away falsehood from your own heart, and then speaking the truth in the Master's way. One thing which will help us to do this in His way is to remember the apostle's reason, "For we are members one of another." We would not wish our eye to lie to our hand or to our ear, or to any other member of our body. Let us cherish that thought. It will help us in our dealings with others.

2. **"Be ye angry."**— The expression is a quotation from Psalm 4:4, not from the Hebrew version, but from the Septuagint. The Septuagint reads: "Be ye angry, and sin not;" but the latter part of the verse is not at all like our Common Version: "Feel compunction upon your beds for what ye say in your hearts." Our Common Version is, "Stand in awe, and sin not: commune with your own heart upon your bed, and be still." The apostle quotes only the first part. There is an anger against sin which it is well for the Christian to cherish. And that anger against sin may be cherished in a proper way without sinning more.

In 2 Corinthians 7:11 the apostle tells us what true repentance wrought in the heart of the penitent Corinthians,—"what earnest care it wrought in you, yea what clearing of yourselves, yea what *indignation*,"— not against individuals, but against sin and the disposition to sin. We may see many deeds of injustice done which arouse our indignation because of the unrighteousness of them, but let not our anger be that which will lead us to sin, or do that which is wrong. Let it be against the deed, with pity for the doer. There may be times when our wrath is stirred because of overflowing wickedness on every side, but let not the sun go down upon it. In other words, take them to the great Burden Bearer. The Greek is "provocation" instead of "wrath." The devil will do all in his power to provoke God's children; but before the day closes, let us settle it with God, and leave it with Him. There is nothing that will undermine health and take away all peace of heart like cherishing a hard spirit, a revengeful spirit, a wrathful spirit, toward others; and there is no other way of truly getting rid of it but by putting it away for the Master's sake, and leaving all with Him.

3. **"Neither give place to the devil."**— In other words, let there be no place in your heart for him. God has cast him out. He has, through the grace of Christ, cleansed the temple. Recall the parable of the Gospels, of the demon that was cast out, and the house swept and garnished, but nothing was put

into the house, and so the demon comes back and brings with him seven others worse than himself. The only means of keeping the devil out of the heart is to let Christ dwell there; as we read in the third chapter, "that Christ may dwell in your hearts through faith." If we desire Christ to dwell there, and in a general way be better than we have been before, but specifically yield to little sins and the things that our natural hearts long for, every one of them that is admitted and cherished gives place to the devil. Every hard feeling which we indulge gives place to the devil. Jesus could truly say that "the prince of the world cometh: and he hath nothing in Me." God and His holy will filled the heart of Jesus. If we would possess His character, free from the power of the enemy, we must let Christ in the heart, that He may fill it. James has told us, "Resist the devil, and he will flee from you." Give him no place.

4. **"Steal no more."**— It was a common thing among some of the heathen nations to make stealing a virtue. Children were taught to steal. The greater wrong seemed to be in being found out, or in getting caught at the stealing. Thus they could better prey upon their enemies, for there was constant war among such. Slaves practised stealing because they felt that injustice was done them continually, and in such way they would get even with their masters. Then, too, stealing stands here as an example of the transgression of every one of God's commandments; and the apostle would have Christians understand that whatever wrong they had been doing in the past, before they knew Christ, they must put all these away now. "Let him that stole steal no more." Let him that used profane language use it no more. Let him that committed adultery do it no more. Let him that worshiped idols refrain from that. And so with every other precept of God. There is a better way to do, and that is to fill heart and mind and hands with the things that are good. Let the thief labor, "working with his hands the thing that is good." Need lies all around him. Let him give to that need of that which he himself has earned.

5. **"No corrupt speech."**— It is an age of corruptness. One hardly knows how common corrupt speech is among some classes. It is common among men where men are together,

and we have been told that in some cases it is not uncommon among women when women are together alone. And one of the sad things is that it gets to be more or less common even in mixed companies and neighborhoods. Sometimes it is indicated by sly and artful suggestions and insinuations, rather than in open speech, and is even more potent for evil than some things grossly corrupt. Let Christians avoid all these things. The speech of men together ought to be as clean and pure as though they were with women. It adds naught to dignity, or strength, or power, or manliness, to indulge in anything save that which is good for edifying, or building up. "Keep thyself pure." 1 Tim. 5:22.

6. **"Grieve not the Holy Spirit."**— Great and powerful is the Spirit of God. By that agency was the earth created and the heavens garnished with beauty. The character of Jesus our Lord was formed and kept by the Eternal Spirit, and by the same is the soul regenerated. Very sensitive is that Spirit. It is because of this that He is able to mold such a difficult thing as a holy character. Do not grieve Him. Mere unconscious roughness will not do that; pain or sickness will not grieve the Spirit of God. Trouble or calamity or misfortune will not do it. But sin will. Sin cherished and sin followed in any form will drive away the mighty Sealer, the one thing which the Christian needs above all things else, because in the Holy Spirit is all the fullness of the Christian's needs. We grieve the Spirit of God sometimes by the things we do not do, by the neglect of reading His voice in the Word, by failing to speak to other souls on the subject which is of more importance than aught else, their eternal salvation; by failure to pray for the Spirit's presence and power.

7. **"Put away."**— The apostle again recurs to the putting away. He takes in the things that are very common indeed among men, things that are not considered very sinful. They are social sins and conventions. Put them away. Put the bitterness away. Cherish none in the heart toward anyone, even though he has wronged you. Put the wrath away, and the anger. Do not clamor for rights or privileges. Do not rail against this one or that one, against the good, or the seeming good. Let all these, and all malice, be put away forever. As

the apostle expresses it elsewhere, "In malice be ye babes, but in mind be men." Children do not cherish malice or ill feelings. Hard feelings go from them like a swiftly passing cloud. Let the Christian cherish the same disposition as regards evil feelings.

8. "And be ye kind."— First of all, "Be ye kind one to another." There are so many rough things in this world, so many hard ways, so many cruel things,

> "So many paths that wind, and wind,
> While just the art of being kind
> Is all the sad world needs."

It is marvelous, the power of kindness. It is discouraging, of course, when kindness has been shown again and again, and there seems to be no response. Nevertheless it pays to be kind,— pays the individual who exercises it, whether anyone else will accept the benefits or not. It develops the character of the Master. Says the psalmist to the Lord whom he worships, "Thy gentleness hath made me great." It is hard, under some circumstances, to be kind and tender-hearted and forgiving, especially when abuse and injustice and blame have been heaped upon us by those against whom we have wrought nothing of evil. But we are not to look to this; we are to look to the One who has had mercy and compassion upon us when we for years perhaps sinned against Him. And so, whatever others may do toward us, we are to forgive,— whether they ask us or not, we are to forgive. "Whensoever ye stand praying," says the Saviour, "forgive, if ye have aught against anyone." And the apostle presses it home, "forgiving each other, . . . even as God also . . . forgave you." This is the teaching of the Lord's Prayer,—"Forgive us our trespasses, as we forgive them that trespass against us."

CHAPTER FIVE

Practical Life: Analysis

I. Imitators of God. Verses 1-12.
II. Foolishness and wisdom. Verses 13-20.
III. Husbands and wives. Verses 22-33.

I. Imitators of God. Verses 1-12.

"Be ye therefore imitators [1] of God, as beloved children; and walk in love, [2] even as Christ also loved you, and gave Himself up for us, an offering and a sacrifice to God for an odor of a sweet smell.

"But fornication, and all uncleanness, or covetousness, let it not even be named [3] among you, as becometh saints; nor filthiness, nor foolish talking, or jesting, which are not befitting: but rather giving of thanks. For this ye know [4] of a surety, that no fornicator, nor unclean person, nor covetous man, who is an idolater, hath any inheritance in the kingdom of Christ and God. Let no man deceive [5] you with empty words: for because of these things cometh the wrath of God upon the sons of disobedience. Be not ye therefore partakers with them; for ye were once darkness, but are now [6] light in the Lord: walk as children of light (for the fruit of the light [7] is in all goodness and righteousness and truth), proving what is well-pleasing unto the Lord; and have no fellowship [8] with the unfruitful works of darkness, but rather even reprove them; for the things which are done by them in secret it is a shame even to speak of."

NOTE AND COMMENT

1. "Be ye therefore imitators."—Our Common Version has "followers." It does not mean a surface imitation, an outward pattern, of the Master. In the first place, that would not touch the real heart and life; and in the second place, it would last only a little while before the hypocrisy would be apparent; for hypocrisy is simply the putting on of a mask; and an endeavor to imitate God while the heart was not in harmony with His will would simply be hypocrisy. Elsewhere the apostle has told us how this must be done,—"And be not fashioned according to this world: but be ye *transformed by the renewing of your mind,* that ye may prove what is the good and acceptable and perfect will of God." Rom. 12:2. And in Ephesians 4:23 we have the same thought,—"and that ye be *renewed in the spirit of your mind.*" The heart must first be made right, for

it is out of the abundance of the heart that the character is molded. Let the instructions given in the previous chapters of Ephesians be carried out, and it is not difficult to become imitators of God, just as the child who loves his father will follow the father; therefore "be ye . . . imitators of God, as beloved children."

2. **"Walk in love."**— Cherish it, develop it by exercising it. Live in its atmosphere by living in Christ. Keep ever before you this one example: "as Christ also loved you, and gave Himself up for us, an offering and a sacrifice to God for an odor of a sweet smell," instead of the stench of sin from us. So live for Him that He, through you, may show forth the same blessed grace and sweetness to the world.

3. **"Not even be named."**— This appeal is further emphasis laid upon what the apostle said in verse 29 of the previous chapter. Do not talk of the things of wickedness, do not talk of the fornications and of the uncleanness and of the covetousness that is going on in the world. Christians do too much of it. "Let it not even be named among you." The heart becomes transformed by that on which it feeds, the mind by that upon which it thinks. It is not becoming to saints, to holy ones of God, to talk of those things that are evil and only evil. Let the filthiness stay where it belongs. There is no need of spotting by it the garments which Christ has made white. Leave the foolish talking and the low jesting, the "lewd turns," as some render. They ought not to be "convenient," as expressed in our Common Version,— better the text which we are using, they "are not befitting." They do not become Christians; they are not an appropriate dress to wear before those outside. They are made by the wrong outfitter. There is one thing that is much more becoming — cherish that — the giving of thanks. Do not grumble. Look upon the bright side. In this way will you commend the religion of the Master.

4. **"For this ye know."**—At least we ought to know it, and every one instructed in the word of God ought to know it, and every one who has had long observation in this sad old world ought to know it,— that no fornicator, nor unclean person — men that give their lives up to such things — have any inher-

itance in the kingdom of Christ and God. They do not have a decent living generally in this world. If they give themselves freely to such indulgences, they become marked, outcasts, even in good, decent worldly society. The wicked themselves feel that such do not belong in the kingdom of God. They would have no taste to be there, anyway; and cherishing those things, they can never hope to get there. A covetous man, we are told, is an idolater. One worships that which he covets. It is possible to covet some things properly. We can earnestly desire the things which God would have us be and possess, but we are not doing that for selfish purposes. The man who covets money, or covets pleasure, or covets lust, so that that coveting becomes the molding thought or power of his life, is as truly an idolater as he who bowed before the image of Baal or Ashtoreth.

5. "Let no man deceive."—There has been, and there is growing now, a libertinism in religion which condones all kinds of sin, just as though God were a great, good-natured king that would pay no attention to the sins, however gross they were. Men are taught that while they are doing these things they are still children of God; all that they need to do is to recognize that fact, straighten up, and in their own strength be somebody; that the germ of life and the relationship with God is there, consequently God will not destroy such, nor allow sin to do it. "Let no man deceive you with empty words." Those who are in sin, in the words of the apostle, are "separate from Christ, alienated from the commonwealth of Israel, and strangers from the covenants of the promise, having no hope and without God in the world." Eph. 2:12. They are "the sons of disobedience," and are "by nature children of wrath." Verses 2, 3. Note where the apostle uses the same earnest exhortation in Galatians 5:21, in which we are told that "they who practise such things shall not inherit the kingdom of God." Also 1 Cor. 6:9, 10.

There is hope for such, however, if they will but turn to God, for such were some of the early saints. The apostle, after naming fornicators and idolaters and adulterers and effeminate and thieves and drunkards and extortioners and revilers, declares, "And such were some of you: but ye were washed, but ye were sanctified, but ye were justified in the name of the Lord Jesus Christ, and in the Spirit of our God." But having been washed and justified, we must not return to the old path. Remember that it is to the disobedient that these things come. But God is able to make the most disobedient into those who love obedience. Therefore because of His love, do not be partakers in such things.

6. "Ye were . . . but are now."— It is well to be reminded of what we once were. Sometimes our hearts get lifted up in foolish pride, and we do not remember the pit whence we were digged, nor the place from which God calls us, and where we all are by nature — unregenerate. "Ye were once darkness, but are now light in the Lord: walk as children of light," and in walking as children of light, prove in your own heart and in your own life what is well pleasing to the Lord. God gives the light in His word. He will write it again in the life, that there may be the twofold witness in His child. Read verses 8 and 10 together, omitting the parenthetical expression of verse 9, which is explanatory of the worth of light.

7. "Fruit of the light."— Verse 9 is a further explanation of the worth of the life that walks in the light; for the fruit of the light is not death, is not corruption, is not ultimate sorrow and pain; it is in all goodness and righteousness and truth. Walking in the light would bring us to the fullness of these blessed characteristics.

8. "Have no fellowship."—A fellow is an equal. Fellowship is equally partaking with the fellows — with other fellows or equals. It is sympathy and comradeship. We are not to understand, by the text, that God would have us utterly cast off those who do not know Him, or turn away from the sinner. That is not the thought of the scripture. Neither would He have us link with the wicked or worldling in fellowship. That is an utterly impossible thing, for we have no sympathy with them in the sin. Our lives should be such that the wicked themselves would know that. But in this darkness of wickedness there are those who are longing for the light of righteousness. There are those who are hungering and thirsting for love. There are those who are longing for freedom from sin and bondage. And if they find those who have no fellowship with such things as that, such a life will be a help and an inspiration and an encouragement to them rather than a discouragement.

We do not win the soul by walking in the wickedness and darkness of that soul. God has lifted His children onto a higher plane than that; but He has given them power and length of arm, by His grace, to stoop down and reach the uplifted hands crying for help in the slough of sin and despond; and He has given power to lift them above the low plane and pit of sin onto the glorious highway of righteousness. Utterly disfellowship the unfruitful works of darkness. Yea, rather even reprove them, if necessary by our words, always by our life. Sometimes silence is more of a reproof than outspoken speech. Let those with whom you fall into association know that when their conversation or acts are contrary to that which is true, and pure, and good, you can not and do not approve of them.

II. "Be Not Foolish, but Wise." Verses 13-20.

"But all things when they are reproved are made manifest by the light: [1] for everything that is made manifest is light. Wherefore He saith, Awake, thou that sleepest, and arise from the dead, and Christ shall shine upon thee.

"Look therefore carefully [2] how ye walk, not as unwise, but as wise; redeeming the time, because the days are evil. Wherefore be ye not foolish, but understand what the will of the Lord is. And be not drunken [3] with wine, wherein is riot, but be filled with the Spirit; speaking one to another [4] in psalms and hymns and spiritual songs, singing and making melody with your heart to the Lord; giving thanks [5] always for all things in the name of our Lord Jesus Christ to God, even the Father; subjecting yourselves one to another in the fear of Christ."

NOTE AND COMMENT

1. "Manifest by the light."— The Common Version has a good thought,—"Whatsoever doth make manifest is light;" that is, it is light which reveals, and anything whatsoever which does reveal the sin is light. Men have learned, in these days of scientific research, that light is not always visible. There are some kinds of rays which can not be seen by the naked eye; but these very rays which the naked eye can not see are themselves marvelously useful in revealing things

which men wish to know. Take, for instance, the X ray, or
the Röntgen ray, by which the bones of the body may be
revealed. What a wonderful help it has been in science! Man
can not with the naked eye discern these rays of light, but the
rays of light can be so used as to make manifest to men things
which the naked eye can not see. This is but an illustration
of the various and many ways which God has of making manifest the good and the evil. The things which are condemned
are made manifest by the light.

It is the light which should be cherished. "Thy word is a
lamp unto my feet, and a light unto my path," says the psalmist. Of Jesus Christ, the One who gives the Word, we read
that He is the "Light of the World." And so God's word cherished in our heart through Him will reveal sin in us, will
cleanse the sin, will make His children what He desires them
to be, the light of the world, revealing by contrast of life and
teaching the world's sin and the world's deformities and the
world's failures and mistakes, and revealing also the clear,
strong righteous way in which God's children should walk.

2. "Look . . . carefully."— Look circumspectly, look all
around, let the feet walk in the plain path, understand and
know the way in which you are walking, not foolishly blunder-
ing into the pitfalls of the enemy, but wisely walking in the
ways of God. *"Redeeming the time,"*— very much better, *"buying up the opportunity,"* margin. The expression is used sometimes of redeeming the days that are past and gone. We can
not do that. "Time" is not used in this text in the sense of
duration. It is used in the sense of opportunity,— this time,
the NOW.

The world has a thousand things for us to do in this time.
The devil will place there a thousand more, if possible; and it
means sacrifice of many things, many times, in order to im-
prove the *now* for God. It means sometimes selling the farm,
and sometimes getting rid of our business, and sometimes
giving up this party of pleasure, or that supper, or one of the
many things which God calls upon His children to sacrifice.
Above all things, it means giving self.

Living a Christian means paying the price, means fellowship with the sufferings of the Lord; but the sacrifice of these

things in the Christian life enables us to buy the opportunity of work for God. There are thousands who are dying spiritually, falling back on the lowlands of unbelief and doubt and sin, who, if they would but yield all that they have to the Lord Jesus, and seize the *now* for work for Him, would find all the blessings which are assured in this our lesson. The days are evil. Let us buy up the opportunity, that we may meet the evil of the days,— buying up the opportunity because the days are evil. It will always cost us something to buy God's opportunities — a pleasure party, an evening of ease, money turned from pleasure to God's work, a new hat, the latest fashion; but so many times these things will buy opportunities to reach some soul in the downward path. It is foolish not to do it; wherefore be not foolish. It is wise to do it; therefore understand what the will of the Lord is, and do that will at any cost.

3. "Be not drunken."— The world is; drunken sometimes with wine, drunken with pleasure, drunken with lust, drunken with all the various intoxicants that men and demons can brew, and out of all these comes riot, comes dissolution of character, comes destruction. Do not yield to these things. The religious may be drunken with the wine of Babylon. There is a better thing to be filled with, and that is the Spirit. Be filled with the Spirit. God waits to pour out His Spirit into the heart that wishes to receive it. See how simple it is! Read Luke the 11th chapter, verses 9-13. "Ask," He tells us, "and it shall be given you; seek, and ye shall find; knock, and it shall be opened unto you." For every one that truly asks, receives; and the man who truly, earnestly, believingly, seeks, finds; and the one that persistently knocks, will find the door opening at last. And then think of the figure which our Lord uses: Will a hungry son ask bread of a father, and get a stone? Will he ask for a fish — a common article of food at the time — and find the father offering him a serpent? Will he ask for an egg, and find a scorpion that is coiled in the form of an egg? No true father would deceive his son, or tantalize him. "If ye then, being evil, know how to give good gifts unto your children, how *much more* shall your heavenly Father give the Holy Spirit to them that ask Him?" "Ask ye of Jehovah rain in the time of the latter rain; . . . and He will give them showers of rain, to every one grass in the field." Zech. 10:1. Be filled with the Spirit. We do not know what joy we are missing when we attempt to satisfy our souls on the wretched, barren husks of this world. We do not know of the joy that would come to us if we were willing to lay them all down at the Master's feet forever, and receive of Him the better, blessed things that would grow better with the use, never pall upon the appetite, and bring immortality at last.

4. **"Speaking one to another"**— the fruitage of the Spirit. How rich the Scriptures would be in such case as that; for there is direct reference to the psalms of the Bible in this expression which the apostle uses, the "psalms," and the "hymns," and the "spiritual songs." Our hearts would be filled with the life of them, and we would talk them and sing them to others. And whether we could sing one single correct note or not, vocally, we would make melody in our hearts to the Lord.

5. **"Giving thanks."**— Receiving such blessings from God, our souls will be filled with thanksgiving. Day by day we would prove Him until we would be willing to give thanks always; and though very disappointing things to the natural heart should come to us, we would give thanks for these also, because He would make these work for our good. And so always for all things would we give thanks in the name of our Lord Jesus Christ. And we would the more willingly work in harmony with others who were like-minded, subjecting or submitting ourselves one to another in the fear of God. And, thus working together, would the church be built up.

III. Husbands and Wives. Verses 22-33.

"Wives, be in subjection unto your own husbands, as unto the Lord. For the husband is the head of the wife, as Christ also is the head of the church, being Himself the Saviour of the body. But as the church is subject to Christ, so let the wives also be to their husbands in everything. Husbands, love your wives, even as Christ also loved the church, and gave Himself up for it; that He might[1] sanctify it, having cleansed it by the washing of water with the word, that He might present the church to Himself a glorious church, not having spot or wrinkle or any such thing; but that it should be holy and without blemish. Even so ought husbands also to love their own wives as their own bodies. He that loveth his own wife loveth himself: for no man ever hated his own flesh; but nourisheth and cherisheth it, even as

Christ also the church;[2] because we are members[3] of His body. For this cause[4] shall a man leave his father and mother, and shall cleave to his wife; and the two shall become one flesh. This mystery is great: but I speak in regard of Christ and of the church. Nevertheless[5] do ye also severally love each one his own wife even as himself; and let the wife see that she fear her husband."

NOTE AND COMMENT

1. "That He might."— We are sure the attentive reader will note that the one motive underlying all these duties should be that of the *fullest unselfishness*. The duty is not that the husband shall *demand* of the wife subjection or obedience. The duty of the wife is not that she shall *demand* of her husband perfect and all-absorbing love. Much of marital difficulty lies right here. The duty of the husband is that he shall *love his wife as Christ loved the church,*— willing to give himself for her, *that he might* be to her, in his own limited measure, what Christ is to the church; *that he might* build her up, beautify her character, honor her as wife and the mother of his children; and so, just as far as it should lie in his power, present her before the world without spot or wrinkle or any such thing. He should love her even as his own body. That is the *husband's duty;* and until he can meet these obligations himself, he has no right to make demands upon his wife.

God has also presented the duty of the wife. She should look to her husband, as the stronger one and the proper one to lead, for help and comfort and counsel. We know no other normal plan, no other regulation, no other setting forth of the true relationship between husband and wife, than that given in the word of God. We believe if the man is a normal man, and the woman is a normal woman, such relationship as that will be natural. The love of the wife on the part of the husband will be whole-hearted, spontaneous, helpful, kind, tender, uplifting, respectful. The love of the wife toward the husband will lead her to do everything in her power to be to him a help. It will not be a *demanding* of the other; it will be on the part of each an unselfish service of love.

One of the great examples that God has given us of this (see 1 Peter 3:6) is Abraham and Sarah. We are told there that "Sarah obeyed Abraham, calling him lord;" but in reading the history of Abraham and Sarah, we find no quarrels, no demands for lordship or ladyship, simply a happy, normal married life, so far as they themselves were concerned. We find Abraham seeking her counsel and following it; and at one time when he did not wish to follow it, the Lord was on Sarah's side, and told him that she spoke truly, and he ought to follow it. All these matters will be settled by the husband's being a noble, strong, manly man, who will do what is right, and regard his wife as a help meet from the Lord, his own equal, and one who stands in her sphere as he does in his, preëminent. The very creation of woman in the beginning teaches equality. God did not take the material from man's head or feet; the woman was to be neither master nor slave. She came from man's side, near his heart, a help fitted for him. The Spirit of God in the heart of each one will fully settle the matter, and settle it in the right way.

2. **"As Christ also . . . the church."**— Our Lord's love for the church is not questioned. He gave Himself for it. He is our model. Even the unconverted man does not hate his own flesh. He would not murder himself, naturally. He ought to love his wife as well as that; and the Christian ought to have for his model his Lord.

3. **"Members."**— Our Common Version has what is clearly a gloss of some of the later Greek copies of the Scripture,— "We are members of His body, of His flesh, and of His bones." The body is composed of flesh and bones, and nothing is added by the use of these terms. "We are members of His body" covers the whole thing. So Christ regards His church, so He cherishes it, so He builds it up.

4. **"For this cause."**— Note that Paul connects the two figures that he is using, the man and his wife, and Christ and His church, and makes spiritual application of the passage in Genesis regarding man and his wife,—man shall leave his father and his mother, and shall cleave to his wife, and the two shall become one flesh. It is the last clause especially that is emphasized in the relationship of Christ to His people. He became one with them. "He is not ashamed to call them brethren." He is a partaker of their flesh and blood. He lived their life

here upon the earth, even washing their feet in His lowly ministry; and though divine and immortal, He is still a brother with His church; and they are still one with Him, even as the head is connected with the members, and the wife with the husband. Remembering this, we shall have more regard for the tender relationship which we have with Him, in the marvelous sympathy which He exercises toward us. The mystery is great — we may not understand that, but we may know that the thing which He expresses is truth.

5. **"Nevertheless."** — The apostle comes back to the family relationship. He would have the very heads of the family themselves in harmony,— the husband and the wife, the husband to love his own wife as himself, and the wife to fear, reverence, regard her husband. Wrong is the idea that some men seem to have, that they are lords of creation, the "head of the household," over whom they can exercise authority as a tyrant. Wrong it is that the man should arrogate to himself, if he is the wage earner or the income gatherer, all of the income, and dole it out in pittances to his wife. She is as truly connected with the work as is he, and ought to have the privilege of exercising a share in the way the product of the firm is expended. It would develop and strengthen the character of the wife, and fit her for heavier responsibilities if they should fall upon her in the future, and it would do the husband's soul good to counsel more with his wife.

A NOBLE PRAYER

If there be a weaker one
Give me strength to help him on;
If a blinder soul there be,
Let me guide him nearer Thee.
Clothe with life the weak intent,
Let me be the thing I meant;
Let me find in Thy employ
Peace that dearer is than joy;
Out of self to love be led,
And to heaven acclimated.

—J. G. Whittier.

CHAPTER SIX

Relationships — Warfare: Analysis

I. Children and servants. Verses 1-9.
II. Warfare, preparation. Verses 10-17.
III. Watchfulness and prayer. Verses 18-24.

I. Children and Servants. Verses 1-9.

"Children,[1] obey your parents in the Lord: for this is right. Honor thy father and mother[2] (which is the first commandment with promise), that it may be well with thee, and thou mayest live long on the earth. And, ye fathers,[3] provoke not your children to wrath: but nurture them in the chastening and admonition of the Lord.

"Servants,[4] be obedient unto them that according to the flesh are your masters, with fear and trembling,[5] in singleness of your heart, as unto Christ; not in the way of eyeservice,[6] as men pleasers; but as servants of Christ, doing the will of God from the heart; with good will doing service, as unto the Lord, and not unto men: knowing[7] that whatsoever good thing each one doeth, the same shall he receive again from the Lord, whether he be bond or free. And, ye masters, do the same things[8] unto them, and forbear threatening: knowing that He who is both their Master and yours is in heaven, and there is no respect of persons with Him."

NOTE AND COMMENT

1. **"Children."**— There is duty laid upon children, and their religion consists largely in that,—"Obey your parents," especially if the parents are godly people. There may be times when it is the duty of the child to obey God rather than the parents; but this is never true unless the parent demands of the child that which is sinful, immoral. The apostle does not leave it unmodified,—"Children, obey your parents,"—but, "Children, obey your parents *in the Lord*: for *this* is right." It is assumed that the godly parent will teach the child godliness, as the Lord has taught it in His word; and as it is the duty of the parent to teach it, it is the duty of the child to obey.

2. **"Honor thy father and mother,"** the fifth commandment spoken by the Lord from heaven, setting forth the duty of children. It should be instilled into their minds from the very beginning. If there were more reverence for the father and

mother, more strict, prompt obedience taught in the home, there would be a great deal less of disobedience to God. A child that was taught to revere his father and his mother would much more quickly learn to revere and obey God. The secret of strong, true characters in the young is in the home. Parents can not escape the responsibility. If they are not willing to meet it now, they will meet it in the judgment. "Which is the first commandment with promise" is a parenthetical clause thrown in by the apostle regarding the commandment itself. Note that obedience brings life. "In the way of righteousness is life; and in the pathway thereof there is no death."

3. **"Ye fathers."**— The fathers have a duty. They may not treat their children as brutes or animals. The children themselves have rights; and one of those rights is that they should be treated reasonably. They are not to be provoked to wrath. Their naturally wrathful or revengeful disposition is not to be stirred up. The fathers should seek to guide and teach by reason and love and example. Children are usually and generally amenable to reason, after the burst of passion is past. They should be taught, nurtured in the chastening and admonition of the Lord, from the time that they are old enough to understand anything,— nay, from before their birth. They may need chastening at times. There is such a thing as sparing the rod when it ought to be used, but it never ought to be used with a spirit of impatience and anger. They should be warned betimes, and admonished as to duty. Sometimes their hearts may rebel against the punishment; but if the punishment be justly administered, with the proper spirit on the part of the parent, it will bring the peaceable fruit of righteousness, and the child will come to see that father or mother did right.

4. **"Servants"**— literally **"bond servants"** (see margin). — This is set over against masters, or lords. It will be noted, by the careful reader of the New Testament, that neither our Lord nor His apostles sought to change social order or conditions. They were not doing politics in the world; they were not forming parties, they were not Republicans, nor Democrats, nor Progressives, nor Socialists; they were just simply Christians, subjects of another kingdom, another empire.

They were bringing down the life of God into the world, and endeavoring to spread abroad the mystery of the gospel of Christ, stronger than all the power of Rome or all the civil governments that have existed. And these very servants — or bond servants — living out the life of the Master even in their slavery, might be the means of winning souls to Christ that they could not have won in any other position in life. Consequently they are enjoined to be obedient to the masters according to the flesh.

5. "With fear and trembling" does not mean that they are to be cringing in their service; but, understanding their duty, they should go about it diligently and with earnestness, keeping before them the great fact that duty is the most solemn and sacred thing that a soul can know. They are to feel that they are not serving some human master; they are to look beyond him, recognizing that when they gave themselves to the Lord Jesus they became His servants, and the service is to be wrought as to Christ.

6. "Not in the way of eyeservice."— That is the way that many in the world serve. If the thing looks well, if they can be seen seemingly to do right work, that is about all that is demanded on the part of the servants. If they can slight their work easily, the work is slighted. They do not know that God sees the part that is slighted, sees behind the hedge, sees where little work and wrong work and imperfect work is done, however it may be covered by men. It is not eyeservice, as men pleasers, but doing the will of God from the heart that God wants. A carpenter was asked, one time, why he finished the pickets of a fence that he put up against the hedge. The one that asked the question remarked that "no man will see that; and the man that you are doing it for will never know it." The only reply was that "God sees it; God will know that those pickets were not finished at all in that place." The true Christian needs no watchman or overseer. He has one thing that he wishes to do, and that is to serve God.

7. "Knowing."— His master may ill-treat him; may pay him insufficient wages. He may even cheat him out of the wages that he agrees to pay. But the servant may *know* that whatsoever good thing he has done he shall receive again from the Lord, whether he be bond or free. In the judgment to come, every wrong will be righted, every deed of iniquity punished.

8. "Ye masters, do the same things."— If truly Christians they are to cherish the same spirit. They are to do as Philemon, the master of Onesimus, was enjoined to do,—receive the slave not as a slave, but as a brother. Philemon 10-16. They are to remember that their own Master, as well as that slave's Master, is in heaven, and that He is "no respecter of persons." The masters who did this were friends to their slaves, and the slaves themselves have loved such masters. The recognition of the one great Master and His love softens and sanctifies all true human relationships.

II. The Whole Armor of God. Verses 10-17.

"Finally, be strong [1] in the Lord, and in the strength of His might. Put on the whole armor [2] of God, that ye may be able to stand against the wiles of the devil. For our wrestling is not [3] against flesh and blood, but against the principalities, against the powers, against the world rulers of this darkness, against the spiritual hosts of wickedness in the heavenly places. Wherefore [4] take up the whole armor of God, that ye may be able to withstand in the evil day, and, having done all, to stand. Stand therefore, having girded [5] your loins with truth, and having put on the breastplate [6] of righteousness, and having shod your feet [7] with the preparation of the gospel of peace; withal taking up the shield of faith, [8] wherewith ye shall be able to quench all the fiery darts of the evil one. And take the helmet [9] of salvation, and the sword [10] of the Spirit, which is the word of God."

NOTE AND COMMENT

1. **"Be strong."**— Literally, be made powerful, be strengthened. The Christian soldier's strength is in his God. He may be as strong as Samson; but, unless he obeys the Master, he will be made as weak as was Samson when he disobeyed. God not only exhorts to strength, He is willing to give it. "They that wait for Jehovah shall renew their strength." Again: "Let him take hold of My strength, that he may make peace with Me." "I have written unto you, young men, because ye are strong, and the word of God abideth in you." Men are made strong by feeding upon the Word, by exercising the strength which they obtain, by prayer to God, keeping the channel of

life open between themselves and the great Giver. God does all that we could ask: "To him that hath no might He increaseth strength." See Isa. 40:29; 1 John 2:14.

2. "The whole armor."—We are not to omit any part of it. The soldier must be clad with the whole armor of God — the apostle makes it emphatic — and only so can he stand against the wiles, not of humanity, but of the devil. There is but one devil, Satan; but many demons.

3. "Our wrestling is not."— Men that fight in this world usually fight against their own flesh and blood. The pugilist in the ring knows something of the man that he is to meet, endeavors to do all that he can to learn his tricks, and to get all the tricks he can that the other man knows nothing about. So it is with the wrestler; so it is with the great armies that are put in the field. But it is not so with the Christian. His fighting is not with men like himself. He might, in such case, have equal part and chance in winning the victory; but his foes are greater than that. They are not flesh and blood, but they are the principalities, the mighty angels which fell. They are the spirit powers that Satan has sent abroad into the world. They are the world rulers of this darkness, Satan's agents who are determining and molding and fashioning the world and worldly governments so as to make it the more difficult for the children of God. These hosts of wickedness are in heavenly places, in the spiritual world. Satan himself is "the prince of the power of the air." In every form, in every way, by every wile which the master of iniquity has used in all the ages, will he still seek to destroy the people of God; and the only way by which the subtle and powerful foe can be met is by the exceeding spiritual power of God, and the Christian panoplied in His armor.

4. "Wherefore"—Wherefore take the *whole* armor, "the full armor of the heavily armed soldier;" take it that ye may be able to stand in the evil day. It may not be to-day, and may not be to-morrow; but it may be next day, and it may be this day. We do not know when the enemy will attack, we do not know when he will let us rest for a while; those who are prepared for the *hour,* and for the *now,* will be prepared for all his attacks. Consequently the armor is not to be laid aside, The soldier himself is to wear it day and night. Having done all on his part, then he may well stand.

5. "Stand . . . girded."— If he is to stand, he must have on the various parts of the armor, and first of all the apostle places truth; that is, the state of the heart answering to God's truth. Truth is the girdle of the loins. That it was which held all the armor in proper place, so as to enable the soldier to fight. Without truth, all the other parts of the armor may be false. All of them may be wrongly bound, and the girdle will break; and the soldier will be slain, or disabled, by his own weapons, unless he have truth for the girdle.

6. "Breastplate."— The armor covering the heart. Righteousness must be in the heart first of all, the seat of the affections, "the breastplate of faith and love." 1 Thess. 5:8. It carries the thought of the love of righteousness. Only as it is in the heart is it worked out in the life.

7. "Having shod your feet."— Not with shoes of war are the feet of the messengers of Christ shod. They do not come to bring war. Christ does not send them out into the world to carry with them war. Men may war against them, and war against the message which they bear, but they themselves must bear the message of peace. The gospel is the gospel of peace to sin-discouraged hearts; but that peace is based in righteousness, and it must be first of all with the throne of God, peace which the world does not give, and peace which the world can not take away. This is the message of peace which God's soldier is to carry. The word "preparation" carries the thought of readiness, and also of firm footing.

8. "Shield of faith."— The shield was formed of metal, or tough rawhide, held on the arm of the soldier, in front of him, which caught the darts or arrows hurled or shot by the enemy. The Christian has the shield of faith. Faith grasps Jesus Christ, his blessed Lord, and faith puts Christ and the invulnerable Word between him and the enemy which may meet him. It is Christ, in such case, that the enemy is to meet, and the soldier fights with his Master.

The shield here described is that of the heavy infantry, oblong, four feet by two and a half, curved on the inner side. Faith places the Lord Jesus in front of us, and no weapon can harm Him. Sometimes the enemy shot darts to which burning tow was tied. See Ps. 7:13. The temptations are shot from a distance. One follows another quickly. Faith in the ever-present Saviour is the only safety.

9. "The helmet."— Salvation is placed in the helmet, and the helmet covers the head. In the modern religion of the day, salvation is generally placed in the heart, and is a matter of feeling. There are thousands who will tell you that they are saved, and they know they are saved, because of the *feeling* which they have in the heart. But next week they are downcast because they do not have the feeling there. Christ is the same, God's salvation is the same, His terms are the same, but the feeling is changeable. What is indicated in placing salvation in the helmet, the helmet covering the head, the seat of the mind? It seems very clear that God would have His children understand that the hope of salvation is an intelligent hope, and the helmet of salvation indicates that the child of God knows that God will save, because he knows that he himself complies with the requirements of the Master, and he knows that the Master's word can not fail.

10. "The sword."— This is the only weapon of offense which the Christian has. All these others are of defense. They clothe and cover the vulnerable parts from the enemy. But he may use the sword, which is the word of God,— the sword of the Spirit. He will find of necessity that many times it will have to be turned into his own heart, to slay the foes which are in the town of Mansoul, which may have yielded to Prince Diabolus. With this he will also meet the enemy when he comes from without. Even so our Lord met him, and when the devil's temptations came to Him, they were met each time with "It is written," a thrust by "the sword of the Spirit." "Thy word," says the psalmist, "have I laid up in my heart, that I might not sin against Thee." "By the word of Thy lips I have kept me from the paths of the destroyer."

III. Watchfulness and Prayer. Verses 18-24.

"With all prayer [1] and supplication praying at all seasons in the Spirit, and watching thereunto in all perseverance and supplication for all the saints, and on my behalf,[2] that utterance may be given unto me in opening my mouth, to make known with boldness the mystery of the gospel, for which I am an ambassador in chains;[3] that in it I may speak boldly, as I ought to speak.

"But that ye also may know my affairs, how I do, Tychicus,[4] the beloved brother and faithful minister in the Lord, shall make known to you all things: whom I have sent unto you for this very purpose, that ye may know our state, and that he may comfort your hearts.

"Peace [5] be to the brethren, and love with faith, from God the Father and the Lord Jesus Christ. Grace [6] be with all them that love our Lord Jesus Christ with a love incorruptible."

NOTE AND COMMENT

1. **"With all prayer."**— How frequently does God impress upon us the fact that we can do nothing without Him! There must be prayer — prayer at all times. A Christian should live ever in the spirit of prayer, praying "at all seasons in the Spirit." This would indicate not always audibly, but with heart lifted to God even in the humdrum everyday work which He has called him to do. God hears the inaudible prayer of the heart that is responsive to His will. See Nehemiah 2:4. Not only praying, but watching "with all perseverance." He must look on every side for danger as well as for victory. He is not only to forget himself, but he is to pray for all the saints. The life must be an unselfish one.

2. **"On my behalf."**—The apostle longed for and deserved the sympathy of his brethren. Note, however, that, prisoner though he is, his chief desire is not that he may be personally blessed, or that temporary ease or prosperity may come to him, but that as he preaches the gospel, he may preach it boldly, as God would have him. So God's ministers should have and hold the prayers of His children everywhere.

3. **"In chains."**— Once again he refers to the fact that he is a prisoner. He does not call it that at this time, but he tells us that he is in chains, or, literally, in a chain. He was bound by the chain to the Roman soldier who watched at his side, but even thus, when examined before the emperor, or in conversation with those that came to see him, he wanted grace

from God and prayers that he might speak boldly as he ought to speak.

4. "Tychicus."—We first read of Tychicus in the twentieth chapter of Acts and the fourth verse. When Paul was on his last missionary journey, there accompanied him, among others from Asia, Tychicus and Trophimus. He was one who was willing to risk something and go with the apostle Paul. Paul calls him a beloved brother and a faithful minister. He knew that the hearts of the brethren would be anxious regarding himself, and so he sends Tychicus, that they might know his state, and that he might comfort and establish their hearts.

5. "Peace."—We come to the close of this great epistle. It has been very briefly and very imperfectly set forth; but we trust that to our readers, to those who have followed these notes and suggestions, there have come some crumbs of comfort from God's wonderful table; that they have gathered some jewels of truth for the casket that shall endure to all eternity; that they have built some moral fiber which shall stand for God in the world's great struggle. Let them be instructed, as they come to the close of the book, that the peace pronounced is to them — peace and love with faith. God is still the God of peace, and the Lord Jesus Christ is still the One through whom it is administered. The only true faith is the faith which works by love; the only true love is that which issues in faithful obedience. And upon such will the abounding grace of God be bestowed; and it is such only that love Jesus Christ with a love which is incorruptible.

6. "Grace."— It is God's wonderful grace, His to us undeserved favor, in the beginning, in the end; it is the riches of His grace all the way; it will be the fruits of "the exceeding riches of His grace" and glory to all eternity.

Studies in the Book of Galatians

Author A. T. Jones' in-depth study on the Book of Galatians, reprinted from the 1899 *Review and Herald* articles.

Studies in the Book of Hebrews

E. J. Waggoner's studies on the Book of Hebrews, given at the 1897 General Conference.

Other Titles from TEACH Services, Inc.

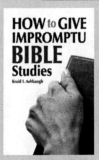

How to Give Impromptu Bible Studies

Kraid Ashbaugh's collection of 24 Bible studies on the core beliefs of the Adventist faith.

Studies on Daniel and Revelation

Kraid Ashbaugh's study of the two main books of Bible prophecy—Daniel and Revelation.

We'd love to have you download our catalog of
titles we publish at:

www.TEACHServices.com

or write or email us your thoughts,
reactions, or criticism about this
or any other book we publish at:

TEACH Services, Inc.
254 Donovan Road
Brushton, NY 12916

info@TEACHServices.com

or you may call us at:

518/358-3494

Produced in partnership with
LNFBooks.com